The Psychology of Human Communication

John Parry

The Psychology of
Human Communication

UNIVERSITY OF LONDON PRESS LTD

SBN 340 11974 8

Third impression 1970
Copyright © 1967 John Parry

University of London Press Ltd
St Paul's House, Warwick Lane, London EC4

Printed and bound in Great Britain by
Cox & Wyman Ltd, London, Fakenham and Reading

Contents

Preface

THE act of communication symbolizes the need of the human subject to maintain contact with his environment and for this reason alone can be seen as supplying one of psychology's central themes. In spite of this, communication has only come into its own as a psychological concept in recent years, and the varieties of human communication have excited very different degrees of interest. Nor has the relationship between these varieties been made at all clear.

To communicate is to transmit a message, but messages are not all of the same type. For the purposes of this inquiry three types are postulated. It will be argued that messages can be the vehicles of signs, of meanings and of affective experiences. This division is made for convenience in discussion and should not be pressed unduly. Border-line cases and ambiguous instances can undoubtedly be found.

Most research on human communication to date has been derived from the invention of man-made systems. Excellent work has come out of this, but few seem to have asked themselves how far this line can take them. Some appear content to go on exploiting the information-theory model without considering the problems that fall outside it, however great their importance.

It is understandable that psychologists should show caution in what they undertake, the more so as full acceptance into the scientific world has not yet been granted to us. But the way to gain this kind of recognition is not by aping the methods of established disciplines uncritically. Scientific method is an evolutionary not a static concept, the stages of its development reflecting the growing complexity of the problems addressed to it.

The physical sciences have been traditionally concerned with measurements of great precision and with prediction at a very high level of confidence. The psychologist who adopts these

9

objectives as the only scientific goals is doomed to a life of disappointment. The reason for this is not hard to see. Man as an adaptive system possesses a versatility far greater than any of the systems he has created, and the price of this versatility is an imprecision in execution which would be unacceptable in a substitute or extension with more limited aims. This means that the goals of prediction and control appropriate to the physical sciences must be modified in relation to the study of the human subject, where prediction at a confidence level which would be useless elsewhere may have very real practical value. There may even be aspects of behaviour that defy prediction altogether. Where measurement is not immediately practicable, it is part of the psychologist's responsibility to ask what comes between him and it, whether the obstacle is in his own approach to his problem or inherent in the theme itself. He must also ask himself whether the requirements of prediction and control are wholly relevant to his theme, and, if it appears that they may not be, whether comprehension and insight may yet serve a purpose.

Because of the mistrust with which psychology was long regarded, the discipline inevitably went through a closed-shop period, during which all opinion unsupported by evidence was ruthlessly rejected. This was a highly desirable tendency, but any tendency can pass into excess, breeding its dogmas and intolerances. Today human problems are so pressing and so various that serious concern with any aspect of them deserves respect, even if the concern is felt by a colleague with a different outlook, or one trained in another discipline, or even perhaps by one who has had no training at all. There are, of course, dangers in too liberal an eclecticism, but it may be doubted if they are greater than commitment to a too restrictive outlook.

The present study sets out first to see how far lines of thought derived from communication theory are likely to take us in the field of human communication, and secondly to outline the problems that may be expected to remain and the sort of attack most likely to further their solution.

Acknowledgements

I WISH to express my gratitude to Sir Cyril Burt for many valuable comments on an earlier draft of this book; to Mr Gilbert Jessup and Mr R. M. Farr who have drawn my attention to numerous important texts and references, and who have read and made suggestions on many of the chapters; to my wife whose experience as a professional artist and writer has helped me in a great variety of ways; and to the Air Force Department for according me six weeks special leave without which it would have been impossible for me to complete the book in the requisite time.

I should also like to thank Miss Sonia Brownell, Messrs Secker & Warburg, Harcourt, Brace & World, Inc. and Brandt & Brandt for permission to quote from *Nineteen Eighty-four*; McGraw-Hill Publishing Company Ltd for permission to reproduce the table on page 137, and the diagram on page 205 from *Language and Communication*; the *Scientific American* for permission to quote from their issue of June 1965; and the u.s. Office of Naval Research for permission to quote from 'The evolution of intelligence: the nervous system as a model of its environment' and from 'Human pattern recognition procedures as related to military recognition problems'.

Of the texts listed in the Bibliography I am specially indebted to Broadbent's *Perception and Communication*, Cherry's 'On the validity of applying communication theory to experimental psychology', Davitz' *The Communication of Emotional Meaning*, Miller's *Language and Communication*, Osgood's 'The nature and measurement of meaning', Pierce's *Symbols, Signals and Noise*, and finally to *Studies in Communication*, a collection of papers assembled by the Communication Research Centre, University College, London.

J.P.

PART ONE

Types of Information

1 Human communication as a theme for psychological study

COMMUNICATION is one of the most complex of human themes, so complex that up to twenty years ago there was very little reference to it in the literature of psychology. It would not be quite true to say that it had suffered total neglect: writers like Stout and Baldwin had foreseen the need for its eventual exploration and had given it a place within the framework of their systems. In the early forties social psychologists became acutely aware of the importance of certain aspects of group communication and did what justice they could to them in terms of existing concepts. But so far as is known, no experiments had been designed to deal explicitly with the human exchange of information before the publication of Shannon's papers on information theory in 1948. Earlier work had often held implications for the theme; Merkel's studies (1885) on the span of apprehension contained many, as, fifty years later, did Bartlett's on remembering. But implication and formulation are not the same thing.

The impetus to systematic inquiry came in the end from disciplines other than psychology, from the efforts of engineers to construct artificial systems and the supporting theory supplied by mathematicians. Wiener's and Shannon's writings excited enormous interest among psychologists in Britain and America, Burt (17)* and Hick (50, 51) being among the first in this country to scent their relevance to human problems. Between 1950 and 1955 a number of experiments were carried out, many of them centring on the time taken by the human subject to acquire information relative to the amount of information gained. At the same time, terms like input, coding, noise, data handling and information processing were released into the bloodstream of psychological discussion, so that for a while it was

* Bracketed numbers after authors' names refer to entries in the Bibliography at the end of the book.

unusual to read an article that made no use of such phrases.

There is, of course, no occasion to mistrust the fertilization of one discipline by analogies drawn from another. The fact that these incursions often come about spontaneously rather than by plan is, if anything, a point in their favour. Planned inter-disciplinary study, though the phrase has acquired high prestige in recent years, is in practice sometimes laboured and sterile. The real points of advance come more often from those unpremeditated leapings over walls sometimes frowned on by the orthodox as bizarre and in doubtful taste.

Since 1950 psychologists have touched communication problems at a number of points, but few if any attempts have been made to set them in relation to one another, to draw as it were a sketch-map of communication as an area of psychological study, showing where effort has been directed and where there are areas that remain untouched. Such a sketch would show intense activity in one highly important region, strong development in a second, moderate but uncoordinated interest in a few others; it would also show regions of great significance almost wholly neglected. It is felt to be time to attempt such a sketch, however difficult its execution may prove to be.

Anyone embarking on an undertaking of this sort must soon come alive to the danger of viewing communication in such wide terms that the theme may lack definition. In the hope of avoiding this, a plan has been chosen which deals successively with four contrasted aspects: varieties of message, barriers to human communication, communication problems in complex activities, and trends in communication research. This approach was dictated in the first place by the need to determine in broad outline how far the application of information theory and its concepts can take us in the elucidation of human problems. At the moment there is a tendency to equate communication studies with these applications, and to brush aside matters that fall outside them. Whatever admiration is felt for the work that information theory has prompted, an attitude of uncritical prostration is clearly unacceptable. For one thing, there appears to be a mathematically unbridgeable gulf between information viewed as uncertainty reduction (the IT concept) and information as content or meaning. But this lacuna does not render all discussion futile, and there are at least two fruitful ways of bringing them into relation. The first starts by noting that while it is not possible to apply the mathematical technique of information theory to content information, most IT concepts have none the less a qualitative significance for information of every kind. It may not be possible to measure accurately the information conveyed by everyday statements about comprehensive schooling, immigration or rent control, but no one can argue that concepts like noise and redundancy lack relevance to the way such statements are made. There must, then, be at least a link between the two kinds of information, and an attempt must be made to see where they meet and where they part company.

The second way of relating the two types of information is by considering the sorts of failure the effort to communicate each can give rise to. It will be seen that transmission failures of the first type can usually be reduced to questions of capacity (the amount the receiver can take in) and interference by noise, while content failures can additionally be due to several new barriers, deriving largely from assumptions (often unconscious) by the sender and differences in mental set between sender and receiver. Thus, a systematic discussion of barriers seems a logical way of continuing the argument. In any event, it is often productive to shift the argument from 'What makes a phenomenon possible?' to 'What interferes with its occurrence?'

With Part 3 the emphasis moves to a series of organized activities—education, medicine, law, etc.—and a consideration of the chief communication problems met with in each setting. The selection of activities, though based to some extent on personal interest and acquaintance, is believed to give a fair idea of the general range of issues.

In the final part an attempt is made to present the main lines of psychological research in the communication field. To do this, it is first necessary to discuss some general notions about scientific methodology and how far these are influenced by the subject matter studied. One of the chief points here is that psychology must not seek to purchase a spurious precision by modelling its aims too closely on those of the physical sciences. If it succumbs to this temptation, it is likely to concentrate its efforts on relatively trivial aspects of behaviour and to wash its hands of the more specifically human. This would be a disaster for psychology and perhaps for history.

B   •   •   •

Before moving into the somewhat abstract world of information theory, it will be sensible to take a quick glance at the communication issues of everyday life. 'How do I get to Charing Cross?' 'Have you a pair of black shoes size 8?' 'What time is the News?' These are questions apparently designed to elicit factual information and nothing else. Each may be regarded as unambiguous in its intention, though it may be noted that varieties of emphasis and intonation can convert the simplest statement or question into a battery of distinguishable messages. '*How* do I get to Charing Cross?' transmits something different from 'How *do* I get to Charing Cross?' or 'How do *I* get to Charing Cross?' This at once raises the question 'Is all information factual?' If the manner of enunciation conveys the speaker's mood as well as his inquiry, do manner and inquiry both qualify as information? It will be argued that at least from the psychological viewpoint they do.

Other common types of communication are the official ('Stand by for an important announcement'), the social ('How are you? I'm fine') and the affective ('Isn't life terrible?'). Most people probably accept these exchanges as facts that give rise to no special problem, regarding communication as a natural activity rather like breathing, and experiencing surprise or amusement when they learn that some effort to convey meaning has led to a grotesque result. There is a tendency to overlook the fact that for every misunderstanding that comes to light, there are probably a dozen that remain undetected. It requires some special event—an important letter, a critical speech—to discover how completely it is possible for words and intentions to miscarry.

There is unhappily a minority for whom communication is always an effort fraught with apprehension. The deeply introverted person is continuously aware of the difficulty of making contact, and much mental illness is permeated by the fear that communication will cease to be possible. At a more sophisticated level we find highly conscious writers and thinkers who hold that communication is an illusion, that words conceal more than they impart, and that all experience is essentially private and untransmissible.

It must not be assumed that all messages are intended to exchange accurate information. Such an ideal is in real life confused by all kinds of cross purposes. Words are used to mislead, to win sympathy, to stimulate antagonism, to bend the hearer to the speaker's purpose. It would not be difficult to make a case for communication as a weapon of attack rather than a medium of exchange. But a study of the purposes communication can be made to serve—though a matter of great importance—is distinct from the study of its anatomy. For whatever moves people to communicate, some transmission of information is implicit, so that the mechanisms of selecting it, imparting it and receiving it will always be involved.

Distinction between literal and metaphorical usage of the word communication is important, if only to keep the scope of inquiry within tolerable limits. Until thirty years ago most people would probably have felt happy to restrict the term to messages sent by one conscious agent to another. But as today's point of departure is the sending of messages through artificial systems, care must be taken. It is true that such systems are designed by conscious agents who are responsible for deciding the type of message that can be sent; so perhaps the reference to these agents is not too far astray. A message from an artificial system designed to transmit that type of message is clearly in a different category from heat 'communicated' to a vehicle standing in the sun or the communication of freight by sea or air. More technically the biologist talks of cells communicating with cells, or even of one part of a cell communicating with another part. For the moment such usages will be regarded as metaphorical.

Throughout this book two or three themes will appear and reappear. The question of how much information the human being can assimilate, whether in a single pulse of attention or by cumulation over longer periods, is basic to all intellectual life. If the subject's capacity for apprehension was half what it is, his life would be impoverished to an almost unrecognizable degree; if it were doubled, it would be lifted into unrealizable dimensions. It is this issue of capacity which supplies the main analogy with the artificial system, always bearing in mind that the human being has developed ways of transcending span limitation in its cruder forms.

The second recurrent theme is the store of information or memory, in the artificial system largely a store in the static sense, in the human being a slow organic accretion which can refine or distort new information and rarely if ever merely records it. The information accepted by a human system has always been selected from a host of competing claimants, and the mechanisms controlling that selection are to be thought of as sets or schemas which human beings are endowed with or in some cases acquire.

The media which transmit information are differentially attuned to its varieties, so that what can be conveyed in a visual medium cannot necessarily be sent in auditory form. As artificial media (radio, press, television) multiply, this matter takes on greater and greater complexity. This issue is relevant to the general question of how information is received from the external world; the case of astronomy, where for centuries all information came through a visual medium and where within the last thirty-five years an entirely new source has become available in radio waves, is a particularly clear illustration, the images of the heavens derived from the two avenues of information having little in common.

Finally, there is the complex relation between communication and expression. The impulse to convey factual information is often rooted in a practical requirement, the human transmitter being uninvolved in the message, except in so far as it falls to him to send it. But there is also a need to express many private experiences, and here it is hard to draw a line between the need to secure understanding and the need to give expression irrespective of response.

2 Artificial and human communication systems

ON the face of it, there is little enough connection between the type of message transmitted through an artificial system and the experience of human communication. There are, indeed, important distinctions which will be made and explored later. But there are also factors which exaggerate the difference. One of these is the fact that the human being is for the most part unaware of the processes implicit in the exchange of everyday messages. He takes the medium of language very much for granted and tends to forget the difficulties he once had in learning the processes (reading, speaking, writing) employed in its use. He is aware from time to time of a desire to communicate, he assumes that where there is a desire there must be a means, and, being more or less aware of what he wishes to convey, he also assumes that the means he chooses will convey his meaning. There are, of course, exceptions: at one extreme the person who is conscious of having failed to master the basic processes, at the other the artist whose work entails continual grappling with a refractory medium. The majority fall into neither of these categories and are only brought up against the difficulties of communication when a new role is adopted, e.g. trying to speak another language, writing an official letter, reading a book on an unfamiliar subject.

One of the processes most commonly suppressed is often referred to as coding, a term that has lately undergone a greatly extended application. The essence of an invented code is agreed correspondence between two sets of items which makes possible the conversion of one set into the terms of another. The need for this is made conscious when it is necessary to conceal the meaning of a message from everyone but the recipient, with whom it will have been agreed that, say, fire stands for drug, auntie for stolen goods, and so on. More systematically, and prosaically, a substitute alphabet can be invented, each letter being displaced a given number of places from its customary position. Codes of this nature are specific devices to meet special circumstances, at school, in war, in diplomacy. Recent applications of the word seem to imply that analogous devices have been agreed by the members of a community and lie behind every message sent. This is noticeably true in language, where it is agreed what words correspond to what objects or processes, and, more basically, what visual signs correspond to what spoken sounds. These language codes are very far from perfect or consistent, but if they lacked any basis of agreement they could clearly not transmit any sort of message at all.

Less conscious still are the means by which the human subject converts impinging stimuli into sensations and perceptions and is able to make cross references from one sense modality to another. Unawareness of this type of process leads people to identify appearances with objects. Obviously these unconsidered forms of coding have not been arrived at by any formal agreement; they must be regarded as products of long evolutionary emergence.

There are important differences between a code consciously devised for a specific purpose and one evolved over thousands or millions of years to serve a wide-ranging choice of goals. A code of the first type will be precise, unambiguous and limited. Being invented to send messages of a clear-cut factual sort, it cannot become a vehicle for generating a new style of message; it cannot be used as an instrument of expression. Its efficiency, like that of the computer, is dependent on human programming and it cannot break the bounds of the programmer's intention. Its signs must remain signs; that is to say, they will possess no connotation, unlike written and spoken words whose use is continuously extending and contracting, and which in a sense may be said to develop their own individual lives.

Compared to a sign code, writing, seen as encoded speech, is on the one hand vague and inefficient, on the other vital and creative. Its vagueness varies from language to language; in English there is a marked lack of consistency between written sign and sound, while it is often surprisingly difficult to frame a sentence free from ambiguity and unwanted association.

The contrast between invented and emergent codes is a special instance of that between closed and open systems, a distinction of great importance to our main argument. Systems devised for specific purposes are usually said to be closed, in that the elements on which they are based have been enumerated and cannot be added to. Alphabets and numerical systems are closed, as are the keyboards of typewriters and pianos, sets of playing cards and chessmen, Basic English and certain types of rating scale. Language in the everyday sense cannot be regarded as closed, since its vocabulary is not finite and the application of words is continually shifting.

Between the clear-cut instances of closed and open there lies a complex position, where a situation can be viewed as theoretically closed and psychologically open. Theoretically, all possible combinations of the letters of a finite alphabet are predictable (provided that a limit is set to the number of elements a single word can contain), but psychologically such a notion has no meaning. A chapter will be devoted to exploring this topic more fully, since it is fundamental to an understanding of human and man-made systems.

3 The growth of communication theory

To communicate is to transmit a message, but a message, unlike a physical entity, cannot travel in its initial form. Transmission calls for a medium in which selected elements correspond to selected features of the original. In many man-made systems the transmission medium consists of electrical impulses, the basic elements being few and simple (short impulse, long impulse, absence of impulse). Nowadays, the basis of most long-range communication systems is the conversion of language (by letter, by word, in some cases by phrase or sentence) into an agreed electrical or typographical code. Common sense suggests that coding should be as easy as possible and that this will be brought about by devices such as assigning the simplest sign (e.g. the single Morse dot) to the commonest feature (the letter 'e'). It is also obvious that speed of transmission and accuracy of reception will be all important to the adoption of an elaborate and expensive system.

In Morse's time (about 1840) a major obstacle to speed was met in the tendency of electrical signals to become attenuated during underground and underwater transmission, and so to overlap one another at reception unless spaced at unacceptably wide intervals. This tendency was largely offset by the use of multiple-current telegraphy, which made it possible to send a number of messages simultaneously.

An obstacle of a different kind was found in the irruption of unwanted electrical impulses. This phenomenon, known as noise, takes two main forms. The more acute is the disturbance arising from transitory but at times violent happenings such as magnetic storms. Less sensational but more persistent are minute undesired currents, comparable to the Brownian motion of tiny particles; these are invariably present. Both varieties of noise have to be accepted as unavoidable, and the designers of systems must secure their objectives in spite of them.

Communication theory took a step forward in 1924 when Nyquist, a mathematician employed by the American Telephone and Telegraph Company, published a paper entitled 'Certain factors affecting telegraph speed'. This sought, among other things, to clarify the relations between the speed of telegraphy and the number of current values. Nyquist expressed this in the formula

$$W = k \log m$$

where W represents the speed of transmission, k is a constant whose value depends on the number of successive current values sent each second, and m is the number of different current values available.

The term current values calls for explanation. Whereas single-current signalling works simply by switching a current on or off, double-current depends on reversing the current's direction. In double-current telegraphy a dot is represented by current flowing into the wire and a dash by current flowing out of the wire; hence at any instant a single message out of two possible messages may be sent. In Edison's (discarded) quadruplex system two messages could be sent simultaneously, one in terms of current direction, one in terms of current intensity, so that choice could be made from four possibilities. Similarly, in a system which permits three simultaneous messages, these will be chosen from eight possible combinations, and so on. This relation between the number of messages sent simultaneously and the number of possible signals (the size of the alphabet from which the particular combination is drawn) lies at the core of later theory.

Thought on these lines was taken a stage further by Hartley, whose paper 'Transmission of information' (1928) introduced the notion of a message-sender as one equipped with a set of symbols (such as the letters of the alphabet) from which he chose one symbol after another, thus generating a sequence rather as a banker spinning a roulette wheel generates a sequence of numbers. Hartley defined H, the information of the message, as the logarithm of the number of possible sequences of symbols and showed that

$$H = n \log s$$

where n represents the number of symbols selected and s the number of different symbols in the set. This reasoning applies perfectly to the roulette example, where each number is independent of the others thrown; if it is to apply to the message-sender without qualification, he must select each symbol at random. In other words, the equation holds only where each symbol is as likely to be selected as every other.

What sort of information can be expressed in a strictly quantitative way? The answer is any information that can be conceived in probability terms. Before each roulette throw, the gambler knows that the next number must be one of thirty-seven. Unless he is clairvoyant or believes the wheel to be biased, he will admit that each number is as likely to be thrown as any other. Until the ball settles his uncertainty remains; the moment it comes to rest the uncertainty is removed. In this context it is easy to agree that the amount of uncertainty removed is identical with the amount of information gained; thus, for information theory information is to be thought of as the reduction of uncertainty.

During the Second World War designs of many communication systems were put forward, and the mathematician Shannon became interested in finding a method for comparing their merits objectively. The problem as he saw it was to decide what sort of signal to send so as best to convey messages of a given type. How could such messages be coded so as to secure the fastest error-free transmission over a given circuit? This is the central problem of information theory, and to answer it with precision it is necessary to find mathematical expression for the characteristic in terms of which different systems can be compared. Let us imagine that two systems for the transmission of English text have been advanced. The first might be based on the idea of coding each word letter by letter; the second on that of assigning a symbol to each word and coding it directly.* If it is assumed that the codes will be in binary form, a fair measure of their relative economy will lie in the number of binary digits (os or 1s) required by each to express a word of average length.

With the second proposal, the number of binary digits to be used for each word will automatically dictate the number of available symbol patterns. Thus, if each word is to be expressed

* This illustration and much else in the chapter is owed to J. R. Pierce, whose *Symbols, Signals and Noise* (88) contains an unusually lucid presentation of information theory.

by four digits, the alphabet cannot produce more than sixteen words, if by five digits, not more than thirty-two words, if by ten digits, not more than 1,024 words. In estimating the size of the required alphabet, it must be remembered that each variant of a verb must have a distinct coding if anything like a normal text is to be transmitted. Hence an alphabet of 1,024 words is not so copious as it sounds; but one of 16,384 words, the number available with fourteen digits, should be enough for most purposes.

How does this compare with letter-by-letter coding? With twenty-six letters, the smallest usable alphabet (thirty-two) will require five digits per letter. The average number of letters in an English word is about 4·5, to which must be added 1 to denote a space. (Space between words must be coded as though it were an additional letter.) Hence, the average number of digits for each word will be 5·5 multiplied by 5, or 27½, which is almost exactly twice as many as the first method required.

This discussion has introduced by implication two new concepts, the binary digit ('bit') and entropy. The bit is sometimes defined as the choice between two equally probable possibilities (0 and 1), so that when a bit of information is acquired, the number of equally probable possibilities has been reduced by half. Thus, the same amount of information is obtained by tossing a coin as by discovering that a number between 0 and a million is above or below the five hundred thousand mark. There is a misleading suggestion of positive substance about the word bit. The concept is really a negative one, which helps by the elimination of irrelevant blocks of signals rather than by pointing a finger at the one to be identified. The bit is in no sense a minimal quantity of information (fractions of a bit are in fact obtainable); it is rather a means of getting maximum information with minimum effort.

The characteristic in terms of which different systems are compared is called entropy, a word borrowed from thermodynamics, where it is used to indicate the degree of unavailability of energy. In information theory it conveys by analogy the degree of uncertainty of information, and this may be expressed by counting the number of steps that have to be gone through to identify a specific item. It was shown just now that two contrasted ways of coding English text needed respectively 14 and 27·5 steps to identify an average word; these numbers express the two systems' levels of entropy. Entropy is designated mathematically by the letter H as used in the simple formula quoted a few pages back.

The broad purpose of information theory is to supply a mathematical technique which helps the designer of a system to strike an acceptable balance between the demands of the message source, the capacity of the channel and the expectation of noise. A successful system will be one where the differences between signals sent and signals received is very small. The flow of a message through a communication channel may be expressed in a diagram:

$$\text{Input} \rightarrow \text{Coding} \rightarrow \text{Channel} \rightarrow \text{Decoding} \rightarrow \text{Output}$$
$$\uparrow$$
$$\text{Noise}$$

So far the discussion has been confined to independent signals, i.e. signals which individually do not influence the probability of their successors. Numerical messages are often of this type, but verbal messages usually contain a measure of redundancy. Whereas the occurrence of a 6 does not as a rule give any clue to the next number, an 's' is more likely to be followed by a 't' than a 'j', while a 'q' is almost certain to be followed by a 'u'. The principles of information theory apply to continuous as well as to discrete signals—their scope would be extremely limited if they did not. But all man-made systems operate with a finite alphabet in which the probability of each element is theoretically calculable, i.e. in a letter code there are known to be twenty-six characters, and the relative frequencies of these in almost any sizeable sample of English text can be determined empirically and found to show very little variation.

The year after the appearance of his famous articles Shannon, in co-authorship with Weaver, published a more general treatment (92). This included a broad interpretation of the scope and meaning of communication as commonly understood. Three levels of communication are postulated:

a) Technical. How accurately can symbols be transmitted?
b) Semantic. How accurately do transmitted symbols convey the intended meaning?
c) Effectiveness. How effectively does the received meaning influence conduct in the way desired?

Information theory is concerned almost exclusively with (*a*) and not with the total range of this. The interpretation is of interest, since it makes clear that the authors adopt more than a restricted technical attitude to communication; they are concerned to show how their own area of study relates to other aspects of the theme. This desire to see the technical in relation to the non-technical and the not-yet-technical is in line with the spirit of the present book.

Whether the language of Shannon's and Weaver's statement does complete justice to all the psychological involvements is another matter. In human communication a great deal of failure comes about not because information has been lost in transmission, but because the sender is unable to express what he has to say, or because the receiver is unable to interpret the message in the way that is intended. The reasons for these failures often have a semantic flavour, but frequently their roots lie in the psychological make-up and condition of one or both parties. Care must be taken not to refer to language as though it were an ambush laid to snare human communicators. Language is a human invention and, if it leads human beings astray, this can only be because they have endowed it with the capacity to do so.

Again, people do not communicate merely to influence each other's conduct; their intentions are often more far-reaching than such a phrase suggests. For example, education, perhaps the most extensive of all communication systems, is designed to produce an informed attitude of mind rather than to bring about specific alterations in behaviour. Thus (*b*) and (*c*) of Shannon's and Weaver's statement are not formulated so as to cover the full range of communication issues. These points will be reverted to later. For the moment we must look at (*a*) to see how far the accuracy of symbol transmission plays a part in human affairs and how closely information theory reflects that part.

4 The human being as an element in an artificial system

D URING the years following the appearance of Shannon's papers, numerous experiments were carried out by psychologists to test the validity of the information-theory model in human situations. These studies have been looked at somewhat askance by engineers and mathematicians, many of whom have taken the view expressed by Pierce (88) that 'while information theory provides a central, universal structure and organization for electrical communication, it constitutes only an attractive area in psychology'. Cherry (25) analyses the matter in considerable detail and reaches much the same conclusion. Both, however, agree on the appropriateness of at least one type of experiment carried out by Hick (51) in this country and Hyman in the United States. In Hick's version, the subject was provided at five-second intervals with visual stimuli derived from one of a number of small lamps to which he had to respond by touching a key corresponding to the lamp in question. When the experimenter varied the number of lamps (and, of course, keys), he found that the response time varied as the logarithm of the size of the set from which the light signal was chosen. In this experiment the light corresponds to the input, the subject to the communication channel and the pressure of the key to the output, the results being noted by an independent external observer. What the experimenter found he could predict was the variation in the rate at which information was transmitted through the subject as the number of possible choices increased or diminished.

Mathematicians are, of course, justified in drawing attention to discrepancies between the conditions of the parent situation for which their model was designed and other situations to which it comes to be applied; indeed, it is necessary to do this in the interests of clarity and sound experimental procedure. When, however, they imply that the value of a model is exhausted the moment a discrepancy is found, it is necessary to dissent. It is true that the experimenter cannot be encouraged to ignore the discrepancy, but he is not called on to jettison the model without further thought. The rational course is to note where the correspondence breaks down and to decide if the deviation is critical.

Scientific and mathematical models are invented to reproduce the salient features of limited ranges of phenomena. But it sometimes happens that a model exerts an influence far beyond its author's intentions. It does this by generating concepts which shape and direct the thought of workers in other fields. Such an influence does more than fascinate and interest; it illuminates fresh areas, and in doing so advances understanding in a positive way. Unless this possibility is conceded, the irruption into psychology of terms like encoding and channel capacity must be dismissed as a meaningless fashion—and, incidentally, the information theorist's talk of entropy would have to be dismissed for the same reason. We must naturally be on our guard against applying the IT model in a confused and bizarre way; nor must we claim that information theory provides the answer to all the problems of human communication. It is obvious that it does nothing of the sort. All that is claimed is that it has offered a foothold on a slope where formerly there was no foothold at all.

Man-made systems are closed in the sense that they operate within the framework of a finite number of possible responses, whereas to all appearance the human being is free in daily communication to shape his answers in any way he likes. He can, however, place himself in situations where the responses to be made are already numbered and specified. The Hick experiment is an instance of this, but such instances are not always confined to the laboratory. Consider the possible answers to these questions and injunctions:

1) What colour am I thinking of?
2) Age last birthday . . .
3) Spurs v. Arsenal.
4) Your bid.

It will be worth examining each of these from the standpoint of three characteristics, which together go a long way to defining the information of closed systems. These characteristics are known as finiteness, discreteness and equiprobability.

Question 1 corresponds fairly closely to the requirements of the second and third of these criteria. The answers invited are discrete in that they are independent of any preceding event and equiprobable unless biased by preference. But they cannot be said to derive from a finite alphabet; there are many ways of designating colour, and unless a particular system has been specified, the range of possible answers is indefinite.

The second question satisfies in respect of finiteness and discreteness, but fails on equiprobability. Even if it is conceded that the ages of all living men fall between 0 and 160, an individual's hesitation in giving his answer will not be due to uncertainty whether he is twelve or ninety-two. It is only within a very narrow zone (two or three years) that comparative probability has any significance.

Questions 3 and 4 presuppose a background knowledge which many do not possess. Without the information necessary to interpret a question's intention, it is hardly possible to decide on the type of answer wanted. Even to the pools enthusiast question 3 might appear ambiguous, since it is not clear whether the required answer is result alone (Home–away–draw), or whether an estimate of goals is called for. When this point has been cleared up, the criterion of finiteness will be satisfied but those of discreteness and equiprobability will not be, since the answers to this type of question may be influenced to an unknown degree by a knowledge of past events.

Question 4 possesses the same formal characteristics as 3, but it is in every way more complex. The number of bids theoretically open to the bridge-player at the start of a hand is thirty-six, so that the number of possible responses is finite; but the choice in a particular situation will be heavily influenced by past events, including the character of the hand dealt. In practice, the bid a player of competence is likely to make is rarely drawn from an alphabet of more than four possibilities, and there are many situations where such players would be almost unanimous (e.g. no bid on a yarborough).

These examples suggest two things. First, while they conform less closely to the IT model than might appear, there is no violence to common sense in thinking of the information they invite as a kind of uncertainty reduction. Secondly, the questions can easily be converted from their present form to something more fully controlled:

1) I am thinking of: A Red   B Green   C Yellow, etc.
2) My present age is: A 18   B 19   C 20
3) The result of Spurs
   v. Arsenal will be: A Home   B Away   C Draw
4) My bid is: A Three no trumps   B Four hearts
                          C Pass

The above form, usually referred to as multiple choice, has been widely used in mental testing, where its employment is often ascribed to the need for objective marking; e.g. in item 1 above the answer A is unambiguous, whereas the word magenta might be accepted as equivalent to red by some markers and rejected by others. Stated in this rather bald way, the explanation slurs the equally important fact that to attain objectivity the question's purpose must have been made unambiguous to the respondent. One way of avoiding ambiguity is by purifying each stream of input information. All systematic thinking consists to a great extent in disengaging informational fibres that have become interwoven. The handling and presentation of data are activities inseparable from all intellectual effort. There is nothing new about this, only about the increased awareness of such processes.

If excuse were still needed for applying the concepts of information theory to the study of human behaviour, it could be provided by the situation where a designer has to decide whether to choose a man or an electronic component to execute some function in his system. If he selects the latter, its maker will have to bear in mind the questions that dominate information theory: can the component transmit at the required rate? How much noise will be inherent? Will the consequent loss of information be acceptable? If such questions have to be faced in designing an artificial component, the assumption must be that they have been met in the 'design' of the human alternative, that the inventor has satisfied himself that the human operator will be able to process information with a speed and accuracy at least equal to the demands of his system. In a general way machines excel human beings in these directions, but there are still occasions where the

c

human operator is preferred. More often the human being is found at a higher level (as commander, pilot or process monitor), acting less as a processor of information than as a receiver of data already processed and in need of integration with data from other sources. However, integration calls among other things for the same skills as processing, so that when quick and accurate decision is needed, the capacity of the human channel is exploited to the full. Thus the principles of sound presentation require that superfluous data shall be eliminated and the essential put forward in the least demanding way. While there is an upper limit to the amount of information a human being can handle, there is, short of it, some scope for manœuvre in determining the presentation that is most effective.

5 The central nervous system as a transmitter of information

ALTHOUGH the theme of perception has probably evoked more words and prompted more experimental work than any other in psychology, its central problem can be stated very simply. It has been formulated by Koffka with the question 'Why do things appear as they do?' The naïve answer, 'Because they are what they are', is inadequate because it assumes perfect correlation, even identity, between object and appearance, and in doing so ignores the fact that a great deal intervenes between the outside world and the subject's impressions of it. The discovery of radio astronomy, already referred to, illustrates on a cosmic scale the danger of premature assumption. Up till 1930 man's knowledge of the sidereal universe was derived from a visual source, not of course from unaided vision, but none the less through a visual medium. On this basis an image of the cosmos had been constructed, an image that obviously went far beyond that of any terrestrial observer, seeing that it supplied all the data then available to astronomers. The discovery of radio waves opened up an entirely new avenue of information, with the result that today's knowledge is built up from two independent sources. The information from these sources is not contradictory, but neither is it redundant; knowledge is acquired from each that has not become accessible through the other. How much more potential information there may be that is not available from either there is clearly no way of answering.

At a very different level, the psychologist studies personality in terms of life data and of behaviour elicited by specially devised tests. Analysis of the data from these two sources has yielded factorial patterns that bear comparatively little resemblance to each other. It can perhaps be argued that fuller data would bring the patterns close together, but there is no sign that they would eventually merge. So much for the assumption that objects are no more than what they appear to be.

Some people, in reaction from the naïvist view of perception, have rushed to the other extreme, arguing that because objects have been shown not to be identifiable with their perception by human beings, these perceptions must be regarded as human inventions. This latter-day subjective idealism is not much nearer the truth than the theory it is meant to replace. No one can seriously imagine that his picture of the environment is a private fantasy, however difficult it may be to demonstrate that it is more than this. Unless he is prepared to deny the existence of other human beings, he must admit that on the whole each human subject finds some sort of consistency in the evidence of his impressions, and that any consistency would be impossible to account for on the private fantasy hypothesis. It is clear, surely, that the alternative to identity between object and perception is something more than a universe of private imagining. The answer to Koffka's question must then be on the lines that things appear as they do both on account of what they are and of what human beings are, that perception is a kind of transaction between subject and object.

Perception figures so large in the literature of psychology because the act of perceiving represents the fundamental link between the subject and his environment; it is thus the basic constituent in human experience. If this is so, the question of what perception is and how it is brought about must lie at the root of man's insight into his own behaviour.

In *Perception and Communication* Broadbent (9) has constructed a model of the nervous system as a mechanism for handling information. Its main features have been dictated by his experimental findings in the field of auditory discrimination, by a comparison of these with findings in the visual field, and by the consideration of both sets of data in the light of information theory. In the final chapter he sets out fourteen principles, the first three of which are as follows:

a) A nervous system acts to some extent as a single communication channel, so that it is meaningful to regard it as having a limited capacity.

b) A selective operation is performed upon the input to this channel, the operation taking the form of selecting information from all sensory events that have some feature in common. Physical features identified as able to act as a basis for this selection include the intensity, pitch and spatial localization of sounds.

c) The selection is not completely random, and the probability of a particular class of events being selected is increased by certain properties of the events and by certain states of the organism.

(d) specifies some of the properties which enhance the probability of selection and (e) offers a theory about the predisposing organic states.

In comparing the nervous system to a communication channel, Broadbent has in mind the central system rather than the initial receptors; the picture is one of a continual bombardment by elements of potential information, each striving for control of the centre. Much of his account is concerned with the mechanisms which decide the elements that end by acquiring this control, but the basic idea is of a central system limited in its capacity for handling incoming information and forced to select rigorously among what is available. This selection must in some way be determined by the subject's need to establish meaning and continuity in his experience; if data were selected on the principle of first come first served, the result would be chaotic discontinuity, there would be no foundation for the growth of long-term memory and no basis for learning and persistent effort.

It is evident that all the information rejected by the central system is not immediately dissipated. If it were, the phenomenon of items retrievable by a sudden switch of attention would present an insoluble mystery. It may be that rejected data is held in a temporary store from which it can be salvaged over a very short period. Short-term memory, as this is called, differs radically from long-term memory; the latter can retain information almost indefinitely after it has passed through the channel, and plays an important part in determining the selection of future incoming information.

Broadbent points out that his statement is largely a presentation in modern dress of phenomena familiar to the introspectionists under the name of span of apprehension, a term used to designate the number of discrete elements (dots seen tachistoscopically, numbers seen or heard serially) which the subject can hold in a single pulse of attention. There is an obvious affinity between the concepts of span and channel capacity, but today's restatement does much to enrich the interpretation. For example, Averbach in an ingenious experiment has shown that the amount of information available to recall during the period immediately following the exposure of a stimulus substantially exceeds that reproduced when a whole report is asked for; in other words, memory span as recorded in a whole report is never more than a part of the information held in short-term storage. Again, rate of gain of information was in a sense implicit in the span concept, but Hick's experiments have added refinement and precision to the original formulation.

While acknowledging that his explanations are in some ways reminiscent of the introspectionist's 'unitariness of attention', Broadbent points out that the introspectionist's conclusion that the subject can only attend to one object at a time is belied by his own findings. What, he claims, limits attention is not the number of objects competing for it but the amount of information entailed. It is quite possible to attend to two objects simultaneously if their combined rate of information falls within the subject's capacity; but if a single object makes demands in excess of this, it becomes impossible to attend even to one.

The analogy between the central nervous system and the channel in a communication system prompts three questions. The first concerns the coding mechanisms within the human channel that control its effective use; we have formed an idea of what these are in man-made systems, and, if the analogy between the two types of system is at all close, it is reasonable to ask how far one reflects the other. The second question concerns the human counterpart of noise. In an artificial system noise is the main factor responsible for information loss; how many forms can this take in the nervous system and what effects does each bring about? Thirdly, there is the question of quantifying information and of what is meant by processing it. The first two of these can be looked at fairly briefly; the third will need a chapter of its own.

Coding mechanisms in the human system

In applying information theory, the designer is asked to accept the limitations of a given channel and the noise that is inevitable with it. He then has to find an alphabet and a form of coding which permits the passage of the desired type of information with minimal loss. If this line of reasoning is applied to the human nervous system, the first objection may well be that human systems have not been designed to handle a specific type of message, that they have evolved over many millions of years in response to an enormous range of environmental changes, and that as a result of this evolution they have acquired a plasticity which helps them to handle a considerable variety of types. This versatility is something quite alien to the man-made system, whose salient characteristic is one-way precision. The point of analogy between the two systems lies solely in the principle of load limitation, within which each can operate with an efficiency appropriate to its tasks. What factors does this efficiency depend on? In the man-made system the criteria are accuracy, which depends on the overcoming of the noise problem, and speed, which depends on the selection of a suitable code—one code is better than another if it transmits a given message with a shorter chain of binary symbols. In the human system, the conversion of impinging stimuli into various modes of perception compels the psychologist to accept the concept of coding as at least partly valid; if he rejects the concept, he is also rejecting the belief that there is any consistent relationship between a stimulus and its representation in consciousness. There is, however, no sense in which the human being can be said to choose his own codes or any evidence that he has ever done so. They would seem to have evolved by trial and error over enormously long periods of time. In addition, the human system appears to possess an initiative which has no counterpart in the artificial system. This shows itself in two ways. First, the central system acts as though it had some power of selection among incoming stimuli; this power, loosely referred to as the power of attention, seems to select information in line with the system's interests and to reject what falls outside them. Secondly, when the limits of apprehension have been reached, human systems can at times transcend this limitation by organizing input elements into more complex units that can in turn become objects of attention, e.g. the digits 1, 0, 6, 6, can, through association with a famous event, be handled as a single unit. Allan has suggested that this organization occurs spontaneously whenever the central system is strained beyond capacity, and it appears possible that the main units of mental life, the perception, the concept and the attitude, may all be to some extent the products of such a mechanism.

Human analogies of noise

Crossman (31) has argued that random variations of behaviour in constant conditions may be due to fluctuations in the brain's nerve-impulse frequency, and that these may be comparable to the Brownian motions of molecules responsible for one of the chief sources of noise in man-made systems. If this is substantiated, it will point to a close basic analogy between noise in the two kinds of system. As we have said, over and above this specific use, the word is applied in communication theory to unwanted stimuli of any sort, such as magnetic storms. This gross type of distraction has many parallels in the circumstances of the individual, whether we think of sound itself and the many forms it can assume, or excesses of heat, cold, vibration or any other environmental factor carried beyond the point where it interferes with the receiving of information. The analogy may be extended still further by including distractors of subjective origin, whether physiological, biochemical or psychological. There is little doubt that the subject's capacity to accept new cognitive material can be adversely affected by pain, shock, grief, anger and anxiety. There, are however, as Broadbent (16) has shown, occasions where noise appears to facilitate the processing of information; there is some evidence that this occurs where a dull task is by itself incapable of adequately arousing the brain centres. In this type of situation noise can sometimes affect performance in the same way as a planned incentive.

6 Information as uncertainty reduction

IT is one aim of this book to distinguish three types of information whose characteristics will be reflected in the messages they give rise to. The first, which will from now on be referred to as sign information, conforms closely to that transmitted in man-made systems. The word sign has been chosen because it carries less suggestion of meaning or content than others that come to mind. Symbol, for example, carries the idea of representativeness as well as of agreed usage; thus, when it is said that the rose is a symbol of love, something more than a convenient substitute of one term for another is intended. But the printed letters of the alphabet are signs which have become attached through convention to the sounds they correspond to. It is true that the word sign has not always been used in this restricted way; words are sometimes referred to as signs, but it will be argued that they carry associations and undertones incompatible with the concept that has to be defined.

The acquisition of sign information has already been described as the measurable removal of uncertainty, and it has been said that a bit of information is attained when the number of equally probable alternatives is halved. But the possibility of measurement does not depend on the alternatives being equally probable; it remains whenever they have known probability loadings. If a biased coin is found to come up heads three times out of four, uncertainty about the outcome of the next toss will be less than if the chances are equal; this can be expressed with numerical precision, the entropy falling from 1 bit per throw when the coin is unbiased to ·811 bits when it is biased in this particular way, since here

$$H = -(\tfrac{1}{4}\log\tfrac{1}{4} + \tfrac{3}{4}\log\tfrac{3}{4})$$
$$= -[(\tfrac{1}{4})(-2) + (\tfrac{3}{4})(-\cdot415)]$$
$$= \cdot811$$

This calculation can be made because entropy is a function of two probabilities, both of which are known. As soon as the probabilities lack numerical precision, expression in terms of bits has to be foregone. On the other hand, the strategy of reduction can be applied whether measurement is possible or not; thus, in a guessing game the intelligent person will approach his goal by progressive elimination of blocks of alternatives, though no one would venture to say how many bits of information are obtained when eliciting that the object thought of is not mineral. Similarly in the more technical field of fault diagnosis: if an electronic system develops a fault, systematic search will usually bring quicker results than attempts to identify the faulty component directly, but it may not be possible to assess the rate at which information is acquired.

What are the psychological conditions that must be observed before sign information can be handled effectively? Since signs are elements in a closed system, it follows as a first necessity that knowledge of the system must be complete. A child cannot handle letters properly before he has mastered the alphabet and incorporated it as part of his long-term memory. Such a system must be known *in toto* or not at all, unlike a language which in a sense can never be known completely. A planned language such as Basic English may offer an exception, but so far as it does so this will be because it is a closed system, incapable of giving expression to new concepts though efficient in handling those with which its authors were familiar.

Thorough knowledge of a system's alphabet is a necessary condition of its effective use, but not always a sufficient one. In real-life situations speed of operation is a second essential. The speed found acceptable will be set by the performance of available human operators, or, where the operator is a component in a man-made system, by the demands set by the rest of the system. If nineteen clerks out of twenty can perform a hundred or more operations an hour accurately, the twentieth with a speed of seventy-five is likely to be found inadequate, however error-free his work may be. But if faster workers cease to be available, the slower man may come into his own. The limitation, in short, is relative. Within the context of an artificial system there is unlikely to be such scope for adaptation; hence the importance of ascertaining as early as possible the demands to be made on a human component.

The essentially active nature of neural substance suggests that the human channel possesses a lower as well as an upper limit to its capacity, a point that may well be related to the human being's intolerance of sensory deprivation. It may also help to explain reported findings about the difficulty of retaining widely separated items in the short-term memory, as well as the undoubted fact that vigilance suffers when signals are received very infrequently. It is as though the nervous system requires a minimum supply of information at all times; where a task fails to provide this, the system will try to make good the defect from its own resources or from irrelevant sources in the environment.

If perception is regarded as an aid to survival forged and elaborated in the evolutionary process, it is easy to think of its first objectives as quick and accurate decision. These are also the goals of man-made communication systems, and it may be that this community of aim is responsible for any closeness of fit between the two types of system. As the human situation develops the emphasis on these goals is to some degree reduced, so that failure in communication at a sophisticated level generally refers to more than a breakdown in split-second response. But though mental calibre may not be judged in these simple terms, the ability to separate relevant from irrelevant factors is essential to high mental achievement.

The selection from incoming stimuli takes place below the level of consciousness, thereby eluding introspection. So far as this selection is dictated by load-carrying limitations in the central system, it seems likely that similar restrictions incline the human being to form concepts as a means of extending his grasp beyond the impressions of the moment. The penalty of conceptual thinking is loss of characterization in the perception of individual objects; it is impossible to isolate the quality common to half a dozen objects and at the same time do justice to the individuality of each one.

The attitude, the affective counterpart of the concept, may well be determined by the limits of central capacity in a similar way. If there were no such limits, the human being would presumably be able to assess each object and occasion in its own right, instead of classifying it in terms of one or two of its more prominent qualities and judging it by these alone.

It is desirable to speak of the acquisition of perceptions,

concepts and attitudes in dynamic terms, that is to say, as points of view achieved with some degree of striving rather than as passive reflections of presented data. The reason we are apt to think of them in the latter way is that having acquired them we tend to automatize them, treating them as habits rather than as continuingly novel experiences. So far as we do this we are using them as though they were signs, but since they are the residue of experiences individually realized, it is not possible to assume the same stability in their reference as with the elements of an agreed code.

The processing of information is a term which has enjoyed a great vogue, and it is proper to ask what is meant by it and how far its use can be pressed. The verb to process is appropriate to any situation where units (objects, items, people) pass in succession through a fixed sequence of stages. In doing this, the units shed their individuality to be treated in terms of a single characteristic: luggage is processed through the customs, spectators through a turnstile, information through a system. The more homogeneous the information, the more fitting the word; for this reason its most natural application is in the setting of a closed system where each unit is discrete and carries no redundancy. But it is customary to apply the term process more widely than this, e.g. to any cognitive activity that goes forward at a regular speed. The reading of straightforward material, in which text is assimilated at a steady rate, can be thought of as primarily a matter of processing; likewise the carrying out of familiar arithmetical operations. We must, however, beware of slipping into the assumption that all mental activity can be reduced to mechanical terms. It may be granted that processing plays a part in any sort of activity, but its importance grows less as the activity becomes more complex. The strain is felt as soon as the speed of intake becomes irregular, assimilation being delayed through the need to re-read, refer and reconsider. Where delays of this sort occur, it is usual to find that an element of learning has entered into the activity over and above the application of habits already learned.

7 Information as content

SOME of those who have written on communication have been inclined to dismiss content information as confused and unmanageable, whereas the concept of uncertainty reduction makes an appeal as measurable, quantifiable and scientific. This attitude would be acceptable in a mathematician, but as the greater part of human converse is a transaction in content, the psychologist cannot disclaim interest in it. If the two kinds of information are in fact irreducibly different, we should at least be concerned to lay bare the roots of the difference between them. As a starting-point we may posit three characteristics of content information which make measurement difficult: first, all content information is connotative; secondly, it need not occur within a closed system; and thirdly its acquisition does not necessarily reduce uncertainty.

1. Connotation is a term used in logic to denote an object and at the same time imply its attributes. The dictionary, for example, describes a goat as a 'hardy lively wanton strong-smelling usually horned and bearded ruminant quadruped'. A description like this goes far beyond denotation. If a man points to an animal and says 'That is a goat' he is denoting it, but the person to whom he addresses the remark is not automatically made aware of all the creature's qualities. It follows that in using the expression 'goat-like' one speaker may have in mind a smell, another a beard and a third licentious behaviour.

A sign possesses denotation but not connotation; it has a function but no attributes. It is in terms of attributes that comparisons and preferences are formed and the majority of day-to-day decisions taken. Thus a farmer is free to decide that no goat shall subsist on his land. But a mathematician cannot rule that no seven shall disfigure his calculations.

This distinction has important consequences. For one thing, a term with a rich connotation is likely to give rise to ambiguity, since there can be no guarantee that in using it the same attributes will be in the minds of speaker and listener. The extent to which this happens even with general concepts like normal and average has been clearly demonstrated by Johnson Abercrombie (1) in her *Anatomy of Judgment*. This risk has caused dismay among philosophers and scientists from the time of Socrates. Many have tried to obviate the risk by establishing fixed connotations for technical terms. These efforts have done much to foster clear thinking, but their conclusion, if pushed to the limit, involves a contradiction. Anyone who says that words shall be used with a single unalterable meaning is turning them into signs and language into a closed system. This can work admirably in the elucidation of a system or model, but it slams the door on phenomena that cannot be assimilated to existing concepts. Thus logical positivism, at one time regarded as the philosophy of scientific method, is in the long view unscientific, because it requires the scientific battles of the future to be fought with the weapons of the past.

Another consequence is that by and large the prediction of man's use of signs is likely to be easier than that of his transmission of content. This point may be studied in the context of the statistical use of language. In writing English text, the author's use of individual letters is for the most part subordinate to his use of words, and certainly of those words that represent the key concepts he is anxious to convey. If we except the writer whose ear requires him to keep down the number of sibilants and the occasional freak who decides to ban a certain letter completely from his work, we may think of the number of 'a's, 'b's and 'c's, etc., distributed throughout a work as sub-behavioural, a matter unrelated to the purpose or quality of the writing. In these conditions it is not surprising to find that the relative incidence of individual letters can be predicted with remarkable accuracy. Their occurrence varies little between one writer and another, between novels and biographies, articles on finance and the contents of the children's corner. Much the same can be said of common words, e.g. conjunctions, articles and prepositions. The picture changes as we turn to substantives, verbs and adjectives. Here some slight evidence of individual differentiation appears, and while no one would pretend that the counting of words brings us within range of the assessment of literary merit, it can sometimes act as a pointer to the themes with which an author is preoccupied. In this situation, and perhaps in others, the highly predictable tends to be the trivial.

2. The second characteristic of content information is that it belongs to open rather than closed systems. This is a feature of all information reached empirically, and it can possibly be argued that the openness is a function of our ignorance rather than anything else. The fact remains that it is rarely possible to say of a class of objects what can be said without hesitation of alphabets and numerical systems: here are the elements of a whole, and it is not possible either to add to them or subtract from them.

3. Thirdly, the acquisition of content information does not invariably remove uncertainty. Uncertainty is to a great degree a function of the mind's preparedness, of the information already in its possession. Where there is no prior information, there can be no doubt. But the absence of doubt does not preclude the acquisition of information. The main factors determining degrees of doubt and uncertainty are the state of information which exists in the minds of different receivers and, more deeply, the mental sets and attitudes which decide whether information shall be accepted and what value shall be given to it.

It was argued earlier that a perception cannot be regarded as the passive image of a ready-made object or as a wholly sub-jective artifact. It represents a transaction between subject and object. This viewpoint is applicable to mental content of all kinds, even the kind it is customary to think of as completely objective. Such content may not be dependent on the private visions of individuals, but it is to some extent affected by the state of understanding men in general have attained. From time to time this state becomes drastically enlarged and revolutionized, and from that moment the facts of yesterday cease to be those of today. The object observed supplies a nucleus of stability, which devel-oping human consciousness surrounds with shifting variations.

In spite of these differences, there are points of resemblance between the transmission of sign and content information. The reception of both kinds of message is conditional upon the load-carrying capacity of the human central system and is subject to interference by the same irrelevant factors. Content information can give rise to the same confusions and misunderstandings as sign messages, but the conditions peculiar to the first are the source of further barriers; these will be discussed in Part 2.

8 Hybrid information

Now that a sharp distinction has been drawn between sign and content information, it is necessary to point out that the two can coexist. To quote Broadbent: 'If I sort an ordinary pack of cards into red and black suits, I shall be much quicker when the red is bright and easily distinguished than when the red is dark and almost black.' In this instance the input comprises information in the IT sense (based on awareness that each card belongs to one of two equiprobable categories) and relations between various stimulus qualities (clear-cut contrast in one pack, difficult distinction in the other). It is easy to see that the distinction between these two strands of information is based on assumptions about the state of knowledge of the sorter. The first strand is said to conform to the conditions of sign information because the sorter knows (a) that every card must be red or black, (b) that the pack contains the same number of red and black cards. If he did not know this, his task would be more difficult; he would be operating in an unfamiliar open system with the possibility of green and blue cards appearing and in ignorance of the ratios between the various colours. No doubt he would end by discovering through a kind of probability learning that the system was a simple closed one, and after that his speed would almost certainly increase.

The question now arises: is it possible to convert the matter of stimulus quality into the terms of a second closed system, and would the difference in difficulty be removed by doing so? The answer to this is rather complicated. Take first the normal pack of cards with clearly contrasted colours. Here it is obvious that red and black have been chosen because of their contrast as the simplest way of setting up a visual code which will distinguish spades–clubs from hearts–diamonds. The colours are thus part of the original closed system and there is no point in trying to regard them as a secondary one.

48

Coming to the pack of cards where the red is almost black, the first comment may well concern the perversity of a manufacturer who chooses contrast effects that provide no contrast. But accepting the *fait accompli*, can anything be done to make the sorter's task easier? Two possibilities come to mind, one very simple, one laborious. The first would be to display to the sorter the 10 of spades (say) and the 10 of hearts before he begins his task and to remark: 'I'm afraid red and black are so alike that you'll find it difficult to tell them apart.' Spurred by this challenge, the sorter may work more quickly and make fewer mistakes than if he had received no forewarning.

The second possibility would be a learning situation in which the psychological interval between the two extremes was bridged by a number of equal stages along the dimension red—red/black —black. It is probable that the speed of discrimination between the smaller intervals could be stepped up by this means, but whether the initial sorting discrepancy could be entirely wiped out could only be decided empirically.

This example suggests that content information can sometimes be converted to the form of sign information by enlarging the area of the subject's understanding, by handing him, as it were, a book of rules to anticipate the partial knowledge derived from experience and to make it unnecessary for him to build up a chain of laboured inferences. Where the purpose of information is to help the human being to avoid ambiguity and to act swiftly and reliably in a thoroughly explored context, there is much to be said for this form of substitution, but it would be an illusion to think of all content as partial and untidy information waiting to be organized into a closed form. Most real-life situations are far too complex for such a breakdown to be possible, and in any case information, once organized, loses its associations, its nuances; the precision it purchases is at the expense of its power to suggest and stimulate to enlarged thinking.

A second form of hybrid information has already been touched on. It occurs where the subject appears to be operating within the confines of a clearly defined system, but where in fact his interests and experiences have so sensitized him to a limited segment of the system that signs have become invested with meaning. Everyday instances of this are anniversaries, lucky numbers,

D

preferences and aversions. In adapting himself to his environment, the human being elaborates a network of orientations with himself as the central co-ordinating point. This elaboration gives emphasis to some features, ignores others, establishes a set of priorities, in which some people and objects rank higher than others and the majority play no part at all. This tendency to endow selected features with meaning and significance persists throughout life and, where the human being is a scientist, must be to some degree in conflict with his resolve to view phenomena impartially and objectively. This does not make it impossible for a man to perform adequately in a mechanized role, but his ability to do so is no guarantee that he will not treat signs as content if he is given the opportunity.

When we ask the day of the month, the date of an historical event, the answer required must be one of a number of alternatives, and the ability to frame the question within the appropriate setting offers proof that the questioner must be aware of the full range of possibilities. None the less, such questions are usually set against a background of knowledge which rules out large areas of these. Thus the questions spring from a comparatively narrow band of expectation, which analysis will find too complex for mathematical expression. A host of hints and associations make a man aware that it is somewhere near the twentieth of the month, whereas car and telephone numbers, at least when heard for the first time, are unencumbered with associations and possess the meaningless purity of nonsense syllables.

9 Information theory as model and as paradigm

ALTHOUGH information theory is essentially a mathematical technique, we cannot overlook the fact that each of its main concepts has qualitative relevance to the transmission of content messages. This suggests that it is based on a way of thinking that is valid in other contexts, where the theory can play the part of a paradigm if not of a model. The implications of this can best be developed by considering each concept in turn.

In an artificial system the term *input* is used of a message as conceived by the sender, i.e. the sequence of words or numbers which he wishes to be placed before the receiver. In framing this message the sender may be influenced by expense, as most of us are when we decide on the content of a telegram. More specific communication systems may limit the sender's vocabulary or even the subject matter; for instance, a policeman on point duty is concerned solely with the flow and control of traffic, and the signs he gives relate to these matters alone. Such considerations define the input in a way which marks it off from the freer input of daily conversation. These markings off are to be thought of as functions of the medium; the purpose of making a telephone call from the United States to England may be much the same as the purpose of calling to one's neighbour over the fence, but the medium of inter-continental communication is likely to exert an influence on the character of the input.

Artificial media affect the nature of input in ways that are mostly dependent on various technical properties they happen to possess. Each medium has its strong and weak transmission characteristics. Visual media are immeasurably stronger than auditory in conveying the essence of a physical movement or the functioning of a piece of equipment, but words come into their own when setting out a theme or developing a chain of reasoning. Another characteristic that differentiates media is the extent to which each medium defines what it is presenting. Those that define with precision are sometimes called hot, while those that invite interpretation from the receiver are said to be cool, a distinction that has been developed by Marshall McLuhan (73) in his *Understanding Media*. The point to be made here is that these differentiations originate as functions of the technical problems entailed in transmission. When a new medium is conceived, it starts with the purpose of aping and extending the range of one already known. The telephone was designed to permit conversation at a distance, television to bring visual and auditory presentations into the home. The ostensible aim was imitation, not the elaboration of new channels with characteristics of their own. In this they differ from the styles of presentation to which the basic human media lend themselves. For example, the style adopted by a speaker in delivering a funeral oration is dictated by his sense of fitness, not by any physical compulsion to speak in a certain way.

The logical extremes of the hot–cool continuum are to be found in sign transmission (which aims to eliminate all risk of ambiguity) and the projective test (which is designed to evoke maximum participation from the human subject). A projective test which elicited the same responses from all subjects would clearly be a contradiction in terms. Thus, ability tests may be classified as hot media—because each item is intended to convey the same requirement to every subject—and personality tests as cool.

Coding serves the purpose of transforming the input into a form in which it can travel; it is balanced by a complementary process, decoding, which reconverts the message from its transmitted to its original form. The defining properties of the code influence what the sender can select as input. He must avoid including material which cannot be coded without ambiguity. A code of this type is essentially a convention in which there is point-by-point correspondence between the elements of input and the elements transmitted.

It has become usual to posit coding processes in many human activities and it is important to be clear how far the analogy holds. How far, for example, is language a code for the expression of thought? If language is a code, how is it possible to express ideas in one language which defy translation into another? Is coding implicit in the relation between stimulus and response? Can one sense modality be encoded in terms of another? The common element in these examples is a partial correspondence between two variables. But partial is not total, and in codes that are consciously contrived the correspondence must be complete. Provided that this is borne in mind, there is no harm in referring to partial correspondence as a form of coding. If it is asked what makes the correspondence partial rather than complete, the answer lies partly in the now-familiar notion that systems that have evolved tend to be open; while, for example, two languages serve roughly the same purpose, the fact that their users inhabit different environments is enough to ensure that their speech structure will diverge in many details. The divergence between two sense modalities is likely to be more fundamental, since on the whole the senses serve distinct functions; the question, then, is not so much why they diverge as why they overlap. To answer this would require a long excursion into neuro-physiology, but it seems clear that total partitioning between the senses would be incompatible with psychic unity. Experience suggests the value of sensory specializations with a considerable degree of interchange and reinforcement.

Capacity or load limitation is the concept round which the analogy between human and man-made systems revolves, but whereas it constitutes a stubborn fact in man-made systems, in the human system it both limits understanding and supplies a basis for higher mental achievement. This apparent contradiction is at the root of many paradoxes. One of these is the aesthetic notion originally put forward by Sir Joshua Reynolds and termed by him 'the principle of unity in variety'. By this he meant that a successful work of art is the elaboration of a basically simple idea, an idea which can be grasped in a flash of attention and consequently must fall within the subject's capacity. Another aspect of this is that while works of art may stir diversified reactions and emotions, the means by which they do so are often found on analysis to be simple and restricted. What is referred to as a painter's or a composer's style can be defined almost as readily in the elements he refrains from using as in the small number he selects to build on. The same point may be made of a spoken language, which is generally developed round a small selection from the many speech sounds available.

Human channel capacity plays a large share in determining the transition from special to general experiences of all kinds, from perception of the single occasion to the formation of general ideas and attitudes. Individuals vary a great deal in their capacity to handle a number of elements simultaneously; on the whole, it is those with a small capacity who find it most difficult to move from the specific to the general. The same limitation exerts a profound influence on the structure of human organizations; it is the factor which makes it necessary to delegate authority and to specialize functions. Psychical economy demands that the administrator be freed from attention to detail, though this does not mean that he can afford to lose his ability to handle it when necessary; one of the hallmarks of the good administrator is his power of detecting the detail of high potential significance, the individual case that may erupt into a major episode.

Noise has already been discussed and some indication given of the variety of interferences that can obstruct the transmission of human messages. In both the literal sense of unwanted sound and the metaphorical sense of irrelevant distraction, noise is an issue of great contemporary significance and one that is too readily swept aside as the product of a neurotic imagination. In considering it, a number of factors should be borne in mind: for example, individuals vary enormously in their sensitivity to stimuli; again, reaction to noise is a product of past exposure as well as sensitivity, and noise histories vary; in addition, a person's liability to distraction varies with the activity he is engaged on, being especially great when he or she is engaged on solitary creative work; and finally, exposure to a moderate amount of noise over long periods is to many people more disturbing (and its effects less easily communicable) than the occasional shattering roar. Research into noise effects for a long time concentrated unduly on the issue of demonstrable physical damage and the possibility of claims for compensation. This is too narrow a conception.

Sign messages are discrete or continuous. The discrete message consists of a chain of signs in which knowledge of the last sign transmitted affords no clue to the identity of the next. Such messages are said to be free of *redundancy*.* Continuous messages,

---

* For an exhaustive treatment of this term the reader is referred to Staniland's *Patterns of Redundancy* (95).

on the other hand, are loaded with redundancy, as are most transmissions of content information. The last phrase is a way of saying that as a statement or narrative unfolds, the hearer becomes progressively alert to its trend or probable ending. In this sense redundancy is inseparable from meaning, carrying none of the stigma imputed by the schoolmaster who writes 'redundant' in the margin of a pupil's essay. Redundancy in this latter sense implies repetition without purpose, but in human intercourse a degree of redundancy is unavoidable. There are only two sorts of message that are wholly free of it: the discrete chain of signs already referred to; and the statement which is made wholly unintelligible through the receiver's ignorance of the language it is expressed in.

As the complexity of a message increases, redundancy assumes a variety of forms. In poetry the repetition of sounds as in rhyming or alliteration is a form of redundancy introduced to secure a positive effect; in Hebrew poetry the practice of presenting the same thought in a sequence of different images achieves a similar end. Metre is redundancy of sound pattern, converted by subtle variations into an intriguing overall rhythm. At a cruder emotional level, all emphasis is a form of energic redundancy employed to convey the message 'Listen, this is important'. The introduction of a visual aid or an anecdote to illustrate a verbal point is made for a similar purpose.

The obverse of redundancy is condensation and cue suppression. Condensation, the packing of distinct meanings into a single image, is, as Freud showed, a common dream mechanism. It is also at the root of much imaginative statement, attaining its most economical expression in the metaphor. Cue suppression is a device for increasing tension. Its success depends on the quickness of reader or audience to supply unstated allusions; there is no golden rule as to how much a writer can afford to omit without losing contact with his listeners. The suppressions and elisions of daily speech suggest a spontaneous tendency in line with the objectives of information theory, namely to transmit a message in the swiftest and surest way. In some circumstances this practice has come to be valued as a stylistic virtue.

10 Closed and open systems

A CLOSED communication system is one in which responses are selected from a finite alphabet and where the probability of each response is calculable. All sign information is based on systems of this sort. With open systems the alphabet is unlimited and probability can be expressed, if at all, only in qualitative terms. Content information is usually of this type, while the human nervous system must for all practical purposes be regarded as open.

As has already been said, some systems which may be presented as theoretically closed must be thought of as psychologically open. Indeed, this is true of the simplest system while it is in the process of being learned. To the learner the alphabet and the numerical system are experienced first as sequences of unrelated elements; it is only when learning is complete and application has become automatic that they can be known as unitary entities and operated efficiently. These systems are acquired not as ends in themselves but as means to a variety of ends. The position is rather different when a code or set of rules is learned for a more specific end, such as the playing of a game. Here the rules may be regarded as one system and the playing of the game as another. It is worth considering each of them in turn.

The rules of a game have much in common with an alphabetical system, but the resemblance must not be pressed too far. An alphabet is learned so that its constituents, the letters, may be combined to form higher units. All written words are combinations of letters, and it is the function of letters to be combined into words; it is barely possible to acquire an extended knowledge of written words without knowing the alphabetical system. While it is necessary to know the rules of a game before playing it, the moves and actions that make up the game are more than a combination of the rules. The course of most games is dictated by an objective which will be stated among the code of rules, the main purpose of the rules being to define how the player may and may not approach this objective. Thus it is the objective that unifies the course of a game, while the unity inherent in the use of an alphabet resides in the system itself. The function of an alphabet is to provide a means of spelling all possible words; the alphabet, therefore, cannot be altered in any detail without considering the repercussions on the rest of the system. Alphabets and numerical systems thus possess a coherence seldom found in the rules of a game. In most pastimes the rules and conditions can to some degree be varied; in other words, they are not mutually dependent. Cricket does not cease to be cricket when the lbw. rule is altered, tennis remains tennis on grass, wood or asphalt. It need hardly be said that for a particular contest to proceed smoothly, the opponents must have agreed on the rules to be observed for that occasion. In this sense the rules may be likened to a closed system; in theory at least no situation can come about for which the rules have not provided. Thus the question raised in the last paragraph is not so much whether a set of rules is closed as whether—since the rules are not always inter-dependent —it should be considered a system.*

The practice of a game as distinct from the compilation of its rules raises deeper psychological issues. All games entail a succession of moves or actions, and in many each move can be accurately described and recorded. This is possible where the player before each move has a number of definable alternatives to choose from, i.e. where an outside observer can list in advance all the things that can possibly be done. This condition holds in most games which do not involve physical participation; in games where there is physical participation it may be possible to list the short-term objectives—smash, half-volley, backhand drive, etc.—but not to define the manner of their execution. This, like the words chosen to answer a question, often evades detailed prediction. Where the alternatives open to a player can be listed, he appears on the face of it to be in a similar position to the operator in a closed-loop system. But does it make psychological sense to talk in this way? The operator's usual task is to transmit signs not of his own choosing; there is no question of

* Piaget (*The Moral Judgement of the Child*) points out that children under 10 regard the rules of a game as inflexible (i.e. closed), whereas older children can accept a particular set of rules as binding for a given occasion.

his displaying initiative within the system of which he is a part. In a game with an opponent there must be continuous alertness to the implications of each response, and, while the player's choice of action may be influenced by past experience so that much of what he does has the character of routine, his interest is dissipated the moment the outcome of the game becomes inevitable. Thus the bridge-player will spread his hand as soon as he knows that his contract can be made, and the chess-player will resign when it is clear that he must be checkmated or agree to draw when it is evident that neither party can force a win. This surely demonstrates that for the player it is the essence of a contest to be open.

The analogy between the games-player and the closed-loop operator is thus seen to be false, but it is worth dwelling on because it illustrates a fallacy very common in scientific reasoning. This fallacy comes about in the following way. All scientific advance depends upon finding an appropriate model. The model will prove appropriate if it reproduces the essential elements of a complex situation in a simplified form. The difficulty is to know whether the features selected are essential; this arises especially when success in one area tempts the research worker to transfer a model to another set of phenomena. To take an obviously absurd instance: the tasks of a typist and a pianist are superficially alike, in that each is required to read a rapid succession of symbols and to transmit them by a manual technique in which fine finger dexterity plays an important role. Observationally and (in a narrow sense) behaviouristically the performances have much in common, and if the aim of the pianist were merely to develop a manual skill, the resemblance would be substantial. The analogy is shattered by the fact that to attain proficiency the typist is required to ignore what the transmitted symbols stand for. To the typist there is no higher goal than to work with the speed and accuracy of a good machine; to the musician there is no more damaging criticism than to be told he plays like one.

11 The role of language in communication

As we have said, it has been customary to attribute communication failure to the snares and ambiguities of language, and there has been more than a suggestion that language is some kind of hostile force equipped to mislead the user. This attitude is an example of the fallacy against which writers on semantics are continually protesting. Language is a human invention and if its systems include features that make for faulty transmission, the origin of these must be looked for in psychology rather than linguistics. The latter may provide invaluable data about the use and evolution of words, but any indwelling tendencies to their misuse are almost bound to have their roots in some kind of human limitation. A phrase like 'the tyranny of words', which a well-known writer chose as the title of a book on communication problems, hypostatizes speech and language in a strangely naïve way. Words are not little demons with blowpipes and poisoned darts, but instruments of thought and expression which can be used well or ill according to the user's percipience.

To get a helpful perspective on language as a communication medium, it is important to ask the right questions. This is not always done. For example, a great deal of effort has been put into the question 'What is the origin of language?', the assumption apparently being made that it must have come about to perform one specific function—whether to imitate natural sounds, to express simple emotions, to advance group activities, to provide a substitute for gesture when the hands are occupied with work, and so on. It is hardly surprising that attempts to reach agreement on this point have failed, for the question rests on a fallacy. It is most unlikely that speech originated to satisfy a single clear-cut function; the belief that it must have done so is the rationalization of a sophisticated twentieth-century thinker retrojecting ideas relevant to present-day inventions. Because current inventions are designed to carry out specific operations, it must not be assumed that the course of evolution was determined by similarly precise aims. It is far more likely that men stumbled on a rudimentary possibility—the possibility of converting sound into voice—and that having done this, the discovery was found to lend itself to a whole range of functions. Just how the possibility of speech was discovered and its articulation set in motion is unlikely ever to be known, but the control of sound by the speech organs must be regarded as the acquisition of a first-magnitude skill in which three factors relevant to the communication theme must be mentioned.

First, the number of individual sounds the human being is capable of producing is greatly in excess of those he uses in speech. Out of a possible repertory of several hundred sounds (phonemes) each language is built from a selection between twenty and fifty. The sounds selected vary from language to language, so that their choice cannot be accounted for in terms of ease of pronunciation; e.g. the short 'i' in Piccadilly plays no part in Italian, though there is no evidence that Italian vocal cords are incapable of pronouncing it. Thus we are presented at the outset with two questions of psychological interest: why a language makes use of only about a tenth of the sounds available to its speakers, and what factors determine the selection of those chosen. On the first point, it may be that the rejection of so many possibilities is linked with the limitations of central channel capacity, that the development of a language exploiting all available sounds would place an intolerable burden on the system responsible for organizing their use. At the same time, the number actually selected is substantially in excess of the span of apprehension, so that the theory makes it necessary to look for smaller group organizations within the total chosen. Possibly such groups may be identified with the main sound types familiar to students of phonetics, namely vowels, fricatives, stops and resonants. These four groups are differentiated from one another through mechanisms of voice production; with vowels the mouth passage is unobstructed, with fricatives the air passage is narrowed, with stops the air is first stopped and then released in an outrush, and with resonants there are whole or partial mouth blockages. Each of these sub-groups may perhaps be regarded as the systematic exploitation of a specialized form of sound production, which has resulted in a spread of sounds that can be held in a single span of attention.

As to the sounds chosen, association and familiarity will always suggest that those of the speaker's tongue are intrinsically easy and natural, and those of other languages difficult. But there is no justification for these beliefs; babies in the first months of life spontaneously produce almost the complete range of language sounds, while many sounds in any speech go through cycles of alteration, so that over the centuries the mother tongue and its dialects cover a larger proportion of the potential repertory. These phenomena do not, however, help to explain the original basis of selection.

The second factor to be noted is that language originated as heard speech and centuries later gave rise to visual recording. It is easy for those who have been taught to read and write from their earliest years to forget that writing is a convention conceived initially as pictorial representation and later developed into an abstract code (cf. the evolution of Sumerian cuneiform and that of Egyptian hieroglyphs first into hieratic and later into demotic script). A visit to a relatively under-developed Asian or African country soon disabuses the traveller of any idea that to each spoken word there corresponds an agreed and correct spelling, while the intelligent native's delight in writing as 'trapped words' reminds us of the vigour and fugitive quality of preliterate language. To a great extent, rules and syntax must be thought of as attempts to impose system upon language, and the same thing may be true to some extent of the division into words. What cannot be explained in this way are the relationships between the sounds selected; these lie at the heart of all spoken language, even though time brings transpositions and modulations into all systems of pronunciation. It seems likely that the invention of writing and the intensified word consciousness to which it gave rise may have forced the users of language to arbitrary decisions which later led to unjustified assumptions about the relation between words and the objects they are meant to refer to. Many who attack language—Ogden and Richards (80), for example—base their criticism on the tendency to identify words with objects. The strength of this tendency is indisputable, whether we think of the magical properties sometimes ascribed to proper names or the emotion generated round abstract terms like truth and freedom. Why is this tendency so powerful? It is not really hard to account for when we reflect that one of language's main functions is to help us to come to terms with our environment; to do this means establishing points of reference and continuity between ourselves and the things and happenings around us. Seen this way, it is the purpose of language to underline what is unchanging by affixing labels to persistent or recurrent elements; by using consistent labels for persons or objects, we reinforce belief in their identity. So long as we have in mind unique persons or objects, no great risk of confusion exists; there is normally little likelihood of a man applying the words 'my father' to anyone other than the original referent.

But the situation becomes troubled as soon as words are applied to general ideas and processes. Whether, for example, a politician's behaviour is democratic or not is a question to which there can be no final answer; the term has become invested with such a range of emotional tone that it is impossible to denote a referent all will accept. Even greater complications arise in our methods of referring to events. Very roughly we classify what we experience as enduring or as changing, that is, as objects or as happenings. We refer to the first by nouns and the second by verbs with the result that when we meet a noun we ascribe to it a corresponding object. But unfortunately we often depart from our own practice, coining substantives (e.g. behaviour, intelligence) where participial description is intended. Such failures can go undetected for a long time, since word usage and sentence structures lull us into over-ready acceptance. These tendencies have long been the bane of analytical philosophers, many of whom have tried to make a hard-and-fast distinction between literary and scientific language. Their efforts have done much to purify thinking, but it is impossible to follow them all the way. We must reject undue austerity in the use of words for the same reason that most people reject it in ethics, where some degree of experimental freedom is generally considered an essential condition for vital living. Similarly, the right to apply old words to new situations is necessary to vital thinking including scientific thinking.

There need, then, be no mystery about our tendency to identify sign and referent, seeing that the initial purpose of a sign is to act as a substitute for the object or event referred to. If all such references were unique no ambiguity would arise, but the labour of specification would be so great that communication would be hopelessly restricted. Once again, the power to extend thought and experience has to be purchased at the risk of ambiguity. This is the real reason why language is apt to mislead, and any attempt to make it foolproof will inevitably reduce its potency.

The third factor of concern to us lies in the means language offers for relating the messages conveyed by different sense media. Synaesthesia is not, of course, a product of language, but if language were not available to express the deliverances of one sense in terms of another, intellectual life would be greatly impaired. This power of mental movement is a mainspring of all creative thinking (simile and metaphor are the best-known mechanisms for expressing such transfers), and it is of interest to note that it provides the starting-point for Osgood's (82, 83) semantic differential, a technique for investigating the nature of content of which more will be said in later chapters.

In considering the development of language we become aware of two important processes. There is first a continuous effort to achieve economy of expression, by elision, by abbreviation, by contraction, by cue suppression, so that language becomes increasingly tense and highly charged. This tendency has something in common with the goals of information theory, with the proviso that in information theory economy can never be paid for by ambiguity, whereas in daily language ambiguity is to some extent tolerated and in literature at times deliberately exploited. It hardly needs to be added that it is the business of language to transmit meaning as directly as possible, whereas artificial systems transmit in coded form elements which only yield meaning when decoded and reassembled.

The second process, which has no counterpart in artificial systems, is the tendency to use language as a tool for extending experience and understanding. This carries two implications. First, we cannot limit the role of language to communication, or anyway to the communication of observed facts; we must admit a second role which may be termed expression. It is in this second role that language influences our thinking and awareness.

Secondly, language, like every other medium, gives rise to its own brand of imagery. Individuals vary in their susceptibility to different modes of imagery, the mental processes of a person in whom one type is outstandingly strong being greatly influenced by it, so that the verbal man will think predominantly in words and will resort to words when he is trying to communicate something new. Similarly, the visual man will turn to pictorial or diagrammatic forms, the kinaesthetic man to mime and gesture. While synaesthesia permits some interplay between the different modalities, we must recognize the gulf that separates the worlds of the visual and the audile and imposes limits on communication between them.

All cognitive modalities are media linking man with his environment. In this relationship man must be assigned the active role, since it is he who stands in need of establishing a relationship. The environment, the external world, is thinkable without man; man is not thinkable without his environment. The various linkages he has evolved are so many ways of relating himself to the world outside him; how far he succeeds in doing this is determined by what he is capable of assimilating. This is true of each sense severally as well as of the senses in combination; it is true also of intellect and the conceptual tools by which it has evolved. Language is the most important of these tools and it is the function of language to grapple with the not-yet-experienced as well as with the familiar. This distinction reflects that between learning and the already learned. Artificial languages are designed to handle the already learned and because of this restriction they can lay claim to efficiency and freedom from ambiguity. With care and discipline natural language can be used to communicate familiar information with reasonable precision, but its primary task is to extend understanding. To carry out this task it requires a freedom to expand and extend itself, and it is the necessity for this freedom that makes its employment hazardous as well as exciting.

12 The communication of affective experience

THE first part of this book sets out to survey the types of message one human being can transmit to another and to put forward a simple and comprehensive scheme in the light of which a wide variety of communication issues can be studied. So far two types of message have been considered, the first a highly abstract kind thrust into the limelight by the invention of artificial systems, the second the much more familiar but somewhat untidy brand we have called content information. In talking of content information we have restricted its range to cognitive material, which leaves an even more varied field for consideration under a third head. The word affective has been chosen to designate this field because its application carries traditional sanction for the whole gamut of non-cognitive experience. Thus, in talking of affective experience, the intention is to include all messages meant to convey the quality of moods, preferences, values, emotions, hedonic tones, strivings, pleasant and unpleasant conditions (physical or mental), volitions and attitudes. If it is said that attempts to convey the quality of some of these conditions are not normally regarded as the transmission of information, the answer is that the transmission of affective content frequently interferes with the reception of cognitive content.

The affective message is bound to be subjectively tinged, and it will help to start by seeing how far this is in itself a complicating factor. We will explore by easy stages, moving from disinterested transmission to messages whose *raison d'être* is the need to find expression for some private experience.

Let us assume first that somebody asks a factual question and is given the information required. In this situation the response, if concise and accurate, approaches the upper limit of cognitive utterance; that is to say, the speaker transmits information without distorting it, adding to it or overlaying it with emotional tone.

Despite the triviality of its subject matter, his message can hold its own with a proposition about the nature of right-angled triangles or whatever may be selected as a prototype of objective statement.

Next, the speaker imparts a piece of information which the recipient has not asked for. He says, 'There was an earthquake in Nicaragua on Thursday.' The giving of unsolicited information need differ from the reply to a question only so far as the first implies a selection and so presumably some kind of interest by the speaker. He might have chosen to give other information or to have transmitted none at all; he did choose to mention Nicaragua. There is, however, no ground for saying that selective interest necessarily distorts the content of a speaker's message, that it adds to or detracts in any way from the information as it existed before this particular communication. It would, in fact, be unfortunate if this were so; it would imply among other things that disinterest was a condition of sound research, a view which not even the most rigorous metalinguist has yet propounded.

Then there is information concerning the speaker himself, for example, 'I've caught a cold.' Here the speaker is obviously the source of the information and there may be no way of confirming the truth of what he says. What he takes to be the onset of a cold may be a psychogenic symptom. But possibilities of this sort merely mean that it may be difficult to find an objective criterion for such a statement; they do not demonstrate that the statements are necessarily unreliable or distorted. Our concern is not with how the speaker comes by information but with how he transmits it, whether he adds to or detracts from its content in doing so. The answer is that he need not.

So far we have argued that a human being may transmit information objectively even when he has reached it by self-communication. But it is equally obvious that he can if he chooses charge the simplest message, even a conventional greeting, with affective tone:

'Conder: Good morning, Mr Whistler. I'm Conder.
Whistler: In that case, Mr Conder, good morning.'

It does not need a diploma in method acting to know that any sequence of words can become the vehicle for an indefinite number of affective messages and that where there is dissonance between content and affective tone, it is the latter that is likely to get through, a point made forcibly by a music hall actress last century in her rendering of 'Abide with me'.

In the oblique affective message there are two cognitive elements running in parallel. If a man says 'I see ICI dropped 1s 6d yesterday', he may be giving the recipient distasteful news about a favoured investment and at the same time conveying his pleasure at the other's distaste. Every affective message contains a cognitive element. A scream of pain or a howl of mirth has its cognitive nucleus: someone has been hurt, someone is amused. How much more is conveyed depends on the expressive powers of the sender and the sensibility of the receiver.

With sign messages reception is dependent on knowledge of the code being used. This knowledge is of an all-or-nothing kind; partial knowledge has no place in such a context. On the other hand, with content messages knowledge is likely to be partial; no one possesses total knowledge of a medium and hardly anyone can be said to know any area of subject matter completely. So far, then, as understanding of a content message depends on background information, the recipient's store will often be too incomplete to ensure total comprehension. This condition is qualified by the existence of certain basic thought processes practised and shared by all, irrespective of temperament or interest. It is impossible to point to a corresponding core of general agreement in respect of affective messages; men vary in mood and temperament, their attitudes differ, there are few if any objects or conditions that everyone likes or dislikes. Hence the possibility of any general interpretation of affective messages is remote. Against this there are always groups of people who share the same assumptions and outlooks and enjoy the same satisfactions; between people so attuned affective understanding can be very great. This theme will be examined more closely in the next part, under the chapter devoted to compatibility and incompatibility of schemas.

Many of the mechanisms used for transmitting affective content can be seen as types of redundancy; this is not surprising if we agree that all such messages have a cognitive basis, so that in superimposing an affective element we are in some way emphasizing or expanding the cognitive content. In saying this we are not trying to explain the former in terms of the latter, as if in affixing a redundancy label we had in some way opened a secret door. But it is of interest that what would pass as superfluity in a cognitive context is often found to be the directest way of expressing powerful affect, and some insight into the character of affective communication may be achieved by noting the forms redundancy can assume.

Let us start with repetition. An Italian, asked the way to the railway station, may gesture with his left arm to a vocal accompaniment of 'Sinistra, sinistra, sinistra, sinistra, sinistra'. The English reserve this style for extremities of grief. Lear, with Cordelia dead in his arms, cries:

'Howl, howl, howl, howl! O, you are men of stones . . .'

and later:

'Thou'lt come no more,
Never, never, never, never, never!'

Selective repetition is a device that can assume many forms as a technique of expression. One consists in repeating a key word or phrase while varying its environment. The musical rondo (A B A C A . . .) is an extreme instance, and poetry abounds in illustrations ('Calm is the morn without a sound, Calm as to suit a calmer grief').

There are, of course, many ways of securing emphasis without literal repetition: italic and heavy type, underlining, raising the voice, reinforcement of a verbal point by illustration or of a visual cartoon by a verbal caption.

Finally we find aesthetic devices aimed to create a musical effect by the selection of words carrying two or three basic sounds:

'There lies a vale in Ida, lovelier
Than all the valleys of Ionian hills . . .'

where the nineteen consonantals include seven 'l's and four 'n's, and where only one sound (the 'd') is unrepeated. A great range of verse effects is obtained by this type of patterning, the interplay of colour and rhythmical feature offering a visual parallel in painting.

·   ·   ·   ·

It remains to ask how far the arousal of affect interferes with the reception of cognitive content. There is little doubt that extreme affect disrupts the intellectual processes in an extreme way, so that a man in a rage may be unable to assimilate fresh information, while anxiety has a way of bending cognitive content to its purpose. But how do cognitive and affective elements interact at more moderate levels? Is there any evidence that mental activity represents a summation of the two types of content? Or that there is an inverse relation between them? At the moment the intermediate stages seem to be unexplored. At the extremes there does appear to be some evidence that heightened perceptual power is at times marked by an absence of affect.

13 Three broad categories of information

THE three types of information that have been discussed represent progressive levels of abstraction derived from the organism's reaction to its environment. The organism can be thought of as a receiver attuned to those aspects of the external world which affect its survival. In the course of evolution specialized types of reception have developed, the most significant from the standpoint of human communication being the distance senses of sight and hearing. It is pointless to ask if the first messages transmitted from one being to another fell neatly into a cognitive or affective category, or whether (like the cry of pain or surprise) they represented a compound of both. We cannot even say whether the basic sounds which, through gradual control by the vocal organs, merged into linguistic skill, originated as attempts at communication of any sort. They may well have begun as side effects of various actions and states, which through the regularity of their appearance were found to hold significance for other organisms. We do not think of the sneeze or the hiccup as attempts to impress our condition upon others, but they do in effect communicate something about us. Grunting, groaning, sniffing and crying may at one time have seemed equally intractable.

The cognitive statement, though it often contains elements of subjectivity the speaker is unaware of, is marked none the less by an abstraction and generality that sets it apart from an affective response. 'Many headaches are the result of eyestrain' is of a different order from 'My head aches fit to bursting', and would be so even if the information it transmits proved to be faulty. The distinction lies in the fact that the general statement makes no attempt to express the quality of the condition, whereas the second tries however crudely to do this. Most people when attempting to convey the quality of a private experience are aware that they are embarking on a difficult and hazardous enterprise; they have no illusions about the ease of communicating what they set out to convey. Everyone is aware that his affective states vary from hour to hour, that it is difficult to recapture the quality of a past condition, let alone to imagine a future one. This holds even at the physiological level of hunger and thirst, pain and discomfort. The man who is conscious of thirst at one moment has difficulty in recalling the sensations the moment his thirst is slaked. If this is so plainly true of the subject's own experiences, it is hardly surprising that he faces the task of arousing such conditions in others with no great expectations of success.

It is different with the communication of cognitive messages, where conviction persists that what can be thought can be conveyed, the basis of this conviction being perhaps that a statement of fact or a line of argument will by and large mean the same thing to the subject himself on different times and occasions. In other words, there is a suggestion of objectivity about the form of cognitive utterances which leads us to expect uniformity of interpretation.

Bartlett has talked of the effort after meaning which characterizes all human reception that involves a strong cognitive element. The roots of this compulsive tendency are complex; the strongest, no doubt, is an aspect of the living being's need to orient itself to whatever situation it finds itself in. This need manifests itself socially in a determination never to appear at a disadvantage, to appear in tune with whatever word is spoken or whatever mood prevails. Such a bias can lead easily to the suppression of questions that might betray ignorance and so to an assumption of understanding that does not exist. Some degree of this is essential in the interests of social lubrication; the man who calls for definitions at a cocktail party is unlikely to be popular with hostesses.

Four broad reasons may be adduced to explain the continual irruption of the subjective into what purports to be an objective style of communication. The first is to do with the selective nature of media. All communication entails a medium, though we are apt to take the commoner ones very much for granted; so much so that we overlook the fact that they are highly selective. This is another way of saying that we identify the object with its image, assuming that all we perceive of an object is all that there is to perceive. Such an assumption could only be justified if the medium reproduced all there was to reproduce without selective bias. But this condition is never met outside a closed artificial system, where we start by postulating all the elements that constitute the system and then devise a code to reproduce them. Thus the Morse code is non-selective because it is planned to represent every letter of the alphabet; but no visual or verbal code can represent an object or event with this completeness. It cannot even be claimed that a visual code represents all that is theoretically visible, or that all the sensory codes to which we have access can present together all that is theoretically perceptible. This cannot be claimed because individuals vary in their acuities and discriminations, so that the notion of perfect vision or perfect pitch is never realized; further, the limitations of central capacity interfere with the perfect exercise of such perceptual powers as men possess.

The second reason is connected with the reference points rooted in long-term memory. New information is promptly referred to such points, though we are seldom conscious of making these references. We think of ourselves as assessing new data in its own right, ignoring that today's perceptions are invariably modified by yesterday's. It follows that everything said by A is qualified by his state of information when he speaks, and that B's reception and interpretation are qualified by B's state. This tendency is brought into the open by projective and semi-projective tests devised to bring about a wide range of response. In doing this, the tests elicit in extreme form tendencies that are always to some degree present. By way of illustration we may cite French's Test of Insight designed to discriminate the relative strengths of the achievement and affiliation motives. The test consists of short statements describing aspects of behaviour typical of different individuals, and the subject is asked to say why a person should behave in that way. For example, 'Bill always lets the other man win' leads some to attribute such conduct to benevolence (positive affiliation motive), and others to attribute it to fear of failure (negative achievement motive). The point that concerns us is that a statement of this sort is cast as a straight piece of information, but while a psychologist might make it without prejudice (i.e. as pure behavioural comment), the majority of speakers would be unlikely to do so. To most people selective comment implies some sort of inference, and the inferences made vary from speaker to speaker. In this sense, an apparent statement of fact often carries entirely different meanings to different hearers.

The third point is connected with the nature of perception. Most people would agree that perception is the prototype, the basic unit of experience, so that the structure of the perceptual act is likely to be reflected in more complex mental activities, including acts of communication. There is also widespread agreement that learning plays an important role in perception and that when learning is complete, habit enters into the reactivation of perception, so that our awareness of familiar objects is coloured more and more by what we believe them to be; in other words, the residual perception that acts as a sign or token of the original experience has suffered erosion and impoverishment. Thus, while the first reactions to a given object may vary from person to person, it is probable that the subsequent decay to which most perceptions are subject will increase the difference yet more. These differences remain for long undetected through the agreement to use a common code of language. There is no doubt that on the whole people apply a term (tree, say) to the same objects, but what variants of tree perception the term conceals are only brought to light when failure in communication is acute.

The fourth source of subjectivity has already been discussed. It stems directly from the fact that our senses and derivative media such as language are links between us and the outside world. We are continually being confronted by unforeseen events to which we must adjust and our awareness of which we need to express; from this it follows that our main instruments of communication must be open systems that lend themselves to representations of what is new. To earn this privilege we must take risks; to refuse to do so is to shut our eyes to the new and unpredicted.

It may seem rather barren that we can only secure freedom from ambiguity when what we communicate possesses no content or meaning, when we are transmitting the signs from which meaning can be extracted rather than meaning itself. Admittedly sign information is a somewhat dehydrated concept; it is because of this that it can provide us with a model that has value in ordering our thoughts in more complex fields. We must, of course, remember that freedom from ambiguity is not the only criterion by which the worth of communication can be judged. The sense of this will become clearer when the problems that arise in a variety of human activities are considered in Part 3.

14 Scientific statement and artistic expression as the main specialist categories

THE two broad categories which have been termed cognitive and affective contain many specialized types of information, two of which deserve special attention.

Scientific information is often contrasted with the information of daily exchange, which is said to be intuitively reached. The basis of this distinction lies in the belief that scientific and technical terms must be purged of all subjectivity, so that any scientist reading a colleague's statement must be in no doubt as to what is intended and must in the extreme case be able to repeat the experiment reported. For this to be possible technical terms must be assigned a fixity of meaning which allows the reader no scope for subjective variation. This view of scientific language has received perhaps its completest expression in the writings of logical positivists.

Carnap (20), expounding the notion of the empirical criterion of meaning, distinguishes between the expressive and the representative functions of language. The arts (lyrical verses, etc.) are cited as instances of the first, science (the system of theoretical knowledge) of the second. So far the distinction is not unlike the one made here between cognitive and affective information, but Carnap proceeds to make a ruthless division which it is impossible to follow. The only statements, he says, that possess sense or meaning are those which are theoretically verifiable; hence almost all statements made outside a scientific context are meaningless, i.e. they may express something, but they do not assert anything. Thus the famous proposition of Thales, 'The essence and principle of the world is water', is said to express something about Thales, but to say nothing capable of objective verification and so to lack sense; the propositions of most other philosophers are disposed of in much the same way. After this summary banishment it is surprising to read three pages later,

'When we look at the historical development of the sciences we see that philosophy has been the mother of them all. One science after another has been detached from philosophy and has become an independent science.' The only conclusion these lines of thought can lead to is that sense is the offspring of non-sense, but it may be doubted if this is what the author intended.

Carnap, though not always logical himself, is quick to detect lapses even in those of his own way of thinking. He points out, for example, that Wittgenstein (115), having asserted that philosophical propositions cannot be stated, concludes with the famous line, 'Whereof one cannot speak, thereof one must be silent.' But, Carnap says, he does not keep silent; he writes a whole philosophical book.

The flaw in Carnap's and Wittgenstein's logic has the same root. Both say correctly enough that some communications are concerned to transmit factual and theoretical information, while others set out to express values and states of mind. Because, however, they are preoccupied with the impeccable scientific statement, they confuse imprecision with affective expression, making a single category of imperfect cognitive statements and all expressive statements, whether precise or otherwise. Part of the trouble lies in the assumption that expressive and representative statements are in all respects mutually exclusive; whereas, in fact, it continually happens that representative statements contain an expressive element, while all expressive statements contain a representative element. In the terminology of this book affective communication always carries some measure of cognitive content, whereas a cognitive communication may be free of affective tincture.

It is, of course, desirable for scientists to speak with as much precision as possible, but the maximal clarity which the logical positivist claims for every scientific statement is rarely met with. Carnap is no doubt justified in saying that the philosopher's propositions are influenced by subjective assumptions, but he is wrong in implying that similar influences play no part in scientific matters. Before a scientist can get to grips with any set of phenomena, he has to view them in a certain way. While he may formulate the hypothesis he is about to test in a perfectly conscious manner, he is never fully aware of all the factors that have led him to frame or select it. What he should be able to claim is that having framed his hypothesis, he makes his observations and inferences objective; but equally the logician may claim that having selected his premises he goes on to make valid deductions. If philosophy and science must be set against one another, it must be in terms of reasoning versus observation rather than subjectivity versus objectivity. It is, however, more profitable to follow Carnap in his liberal mood by regarding dialectic (the product of philosophy) as the first stage in scientific thinking, empirical observation as the second stage, controlled experiment as the third, and systematic prediction as the fourth. In this way disciplined thinking can be seen as an instrument forged over the centuries to bring human beings into more intimate relation with their environment.

The ideal of objectivity exalted by Carnap and his associates is really an attempt to convert scientific language to the category of pure signs, that is, to impose on each term an unvarying meaning. This is sometimes possible when developing the implications of an appropriate model, but radical contributions to knowledge usually call for something more. They are apt to demand the forging of a new model, sometimes one of a very fundamental kind. When we examine the processes by which these reconceptions are brought about, we find that the creative scientist invents new terms or at least uses existing terms in a new way. In doing this, he often invokes the same mechanisms as the imaginative artist, dealing in metaphors and analogies, relating the situations he is examining to situations in remote fields. He may or may not employ words to do this; there is evidence that many of the great innovators (Faraday, Clerk Maxwell, Einstein) used visual and at times kinaesthetic imagery almost exclusively, and that verbal concepts played a very minor role in their achievement. This aspect of scientific discovery has been explored and documented by a number of writers including Koestler (62) whose *Act of Creation* brings together a great deal of relevant data.

The sharp distinction between objective and subjective is an instance of the dichotomous thinking which elsewhere is condemned. A more sophisticated approach is to imagine a continuum whose extremes correspond to chance opinion and assertions from which chance has been eliminated, the intervening stages being marked by enhanced levels of probability. The notion of a scientist whose statements contain no element of risk-taking is ultimately a barren one that confines attention to the known and the trivial. All scientific advance begins in speculation; to persist in speculation when empirical verification has become a possibility is undoubtedly a negation of science, but so is persistence in a line of attack whose utility has been exhausted.

In calling artistic work a form of affective communication, we must repeat that the latter invariably contains a cognitive element. No bigger mistake could be made than to assume that the artist's exclusive purpose is to arouse affect. He may or may not wish to do so, but, even when he does, he is faced continuously with the problem of manipulating cognitive mechanisms, organizing his material in such a way that his reader or hearer is receptive to his design. If we examine the structure of a narrative or a piece of music, we find that the ground plan often bears a close resemblance to that of a reasoned argument; the outline of sonata form, for example, has points in common with the dialectical process as described by Hegel. It is as though all intellectual processes require the interplay of contrasted themes, whether we call them first and second subject or thesis and antithesis, and much of the pleasure derived from some forms of art plainly lies in unravelling a cognitive tangle—what Empson has called the crossword element.

It would be equally misleading to try to explain the appeal of art exclusively in intellectual terms. Literature, painting and music stir an extraordinary profusion of emotions, and while some of them may be incidental to the artist's intention, this is certainly not true of all. But it is unprofitable to attempt to specify such emotions in everyday terms; whatever experiences a work of art evokes have been aroused through an aesthetic medium, and, apart from this, the attitude of the receiver is of a special and complex type.

Responses to a work of art can be placed at many points upon the line linking the extremes of affect and cognition. At one pole we find the emotional orgiast who regards music and poetry as passports to ecstatic feeling, at the other the busy dissector armed with score or notebook. It is seldom that the artist himself adopts either of these attitudes or wishes his audience to do so. He is usually a workman highly conscious of the effects he wants to produce and though his work may be sustained by an imaginative conception, he is bound to be concerned a great deal of the time with detailed practical problems. Does it sound better this way or that? Is this word precise enough? Is the meaning here too obvious? If this cue is removed, will the reader know what I am talking about? Much creative activity can be seen as a running sequence of questions and answers, and in this respect the artist's work may be compared to the experimental scientist's. Such a critical approach involves the cognitive faculties throughout; whatever excitement the artist may experience and whatever state of mind his work may induce, the process of bringing it into existence is usually one of acute awareness.

While there are points of resemblance between the scientist's and artist's activities, no purpose is served by seeking to identify them. They differ radically in a number of ways. To begin with, the criterion of scientific effort is external; a hypothesis is proved or disproved and the possibility of prediction is dependent on establishing a better than chance relation between hypothesis and experimental finding. The artist's criterion (if the word is appropriate) is internal to his purpose; he creates objects whose justification is self-contained. If validity can be applied in this context at all, it relates to the artist's success in realizing his intention.

Again, a work of art is unique in that different artists never produce the same book or the same painting. But though the work of scientists may bear the stamp of their personalities, and although the processes of the most original scientists are rightly called creative, it is not unusual for two or more scientists to make the same discovery independently: Newton and Leibniz (the calculus), Darwin and Wallace (evolution), Adams and Leverrier (the planet Neptune).

Finally, while a scientific proof or experiment may be said to exert an aesthetic appeal, this is incidental to its purpose, whereas the attitude that leads to aesthetic experience is part and parcel of artistic enterprise. This attitude entails both detachment and involvement: detachment in that the experient has no designs on the work, whether to use it or sell it; involvement in that the experience commands attention and excites admiration.

These specialized forms of communication receive fuller treatment in Part 3; they are touched on here to round off the sketch of informational varieties with which this opening part has been concerned.

A note on the measurement of information

Once the concept of information measurement has been accepted, we see that there is not a single dimension but many, just as there are many ways of measuring the physical attributes of human beings. The term was used as long ago as 1934 by R. A. Fisher, but in coining it Fisher was concerned with a totally different problem from Shannon fifteen years later. Shannon's line of interest was, in turn, remote from Osgood's when the latter laid the foundations of semantic differential theory about 1951. Semantic differential theory is a technique for exploring the anatomy of verbal meaning, and this again is unrelated to the problem of measuring the 'amount' of meaning transmitted in a content message. This last problem has received so little attention that it is still hard to place it in a mathematical perspective. Almost the only attempt to do so is to be found in a letter to *Nature* by the late C. C. L. Gregory (44), founder of the Institute for the Study of Mental Images. The purpose of this letter is to adumbrate a bridge linking Eddington's thinking about basic entities with the language of communication theory. Eddington conceived the most primitive entities in terms of two attributes only, existence and non-existence; this, in Gregory's submission, can be represented by one binomial unit of information (one bit). Eddington's second-level entity, the observable, is represented by two entities and has four characteristics, and his third-level, the measurable, by two observables (or four entities) with sixteen characteristics. 'This means that an entity has one way of not existing out of two possibilities, an observable three ways out of four, and a measurable fifteen ways out of sixteen.' Gregory's own contribution is the concept of a comparable, intermediate between an observable and a measurable. 'A comparable is represented by three bits of information, has eight characteristics, and accordingly it has seven ways of not existing within this universe of discourse.' Gregory adds: 'So long as science is based upon measurables, its primitives must be measurable things, that is, atoms, but if a science is based upon comparables, this allows comparisons to be made between an observable entity, such as a semantic relationship, with an observable such as a physiological response. Luria's work along these lines makes meaning observable, but not measurable in the physical sense, and so, in principle, separates meaning from knowledge in just the same way as the cybernetic engineer separates information from meaning.'

This argument appears to run counter to the views of most psychologists, including those of the present writer. The letter is, however, believed to have elicited no formal comment or refutation.

PART TWO

Barriers to Human Communication

COMMUNICATION, like many other human themes, can be viewed as a mystery whose solution offers a challenge to the inquirer, or as a natural happening whose failures are equally in need of explanation. Research can proceed from either of these positions; the first stream is likely to appear as a search for basic principles in terms of which the chief manifestations of the activity become comprehensible, the second as a series of attempts to grapple with practical individual problems. Frequently these lines develop over long periods with little contact or interplay; for example, the standard works on learning theory make little reference to the prolonged efforts of Piaget and other educational psychologists to study the developmental phases of children's intellectual growth. The first part of this book has inclined to the more basic questions: how is communication between persons possible? What different kinds of communication are to be distinguished? And we have seen that the impulse to such questions has come largely from the invention of artificial communication systems. In this second part we shall be adopting more of a practitioner's role, accepting attempts at inter-personal communication as natural and largely successful, and turning our attention to the factors that thwart it.

15 The seven barriers named

THERE are seven main barriers to human communication:
1) Limitation of the receiver's capacity.
2) Distraction (noise).
3) The unstated assumption.
4) Incompatibility of schemas.
5) Intrusion of unconscious or partly conscious mechanisms.
6) Confused presentation.
7) Absence of communication facilities.

Each of these obstacles to understanding can take a variety of forms, some of which will be set out in the following chapters. The list is no more than an attempt to give orientation for further study; there is no suggestion that the headings represent the outcome of systematic research or statistical analysis. They are put forward as aids to pinpointing the source of specific misunderstandings, rather as a list of fallacies can be of value in tracking down invalidities of argument.

Not all failures of communication entail specific misunderstanding; many do not lead to understanding of any sort, merely to a confused impression that something has failed to register. At other times there is a reduced efficiency in the speed or accuracy with which information is assimilated. These losses can result from any of the first five barriers, but there are additional causes which are subsumed under the heading 'confused presentation'.

The first six headings postulate a situation where a sender is trying to convey a message to a recipient, the failure being traceable to one or the other parties or possibly to both. The seventh is not a psychological conception; that is to say, the failures it gives rise to are unrelated to the characteristics of sender or receiver. It is included partly for completeness, but also because social psychologists and sociologists are highly sensitized to the detection of inadequate communication facilities and still more to the havoc the absence of these facilities can bring about.

16 Limitation of the receiver's capacity

THE phrase 'loss of information' suggests a mechanical deficit, such as the leakage of water from a pipe. This is in some ways an apt enough description of the faults that occur in man-made systems: X signals are transmitted, Y get lost through noise or some other cause, X minus Y are received. But when a human receiver loses information, the effects are seldom as straightforward as this. They are complicated by the fact that the receiver is likely to be aware that information is being lost and to react accordingly. The manner of his reaction will be influenced by the nature of the information. If this is of the sign variety (i.e. without connotation), mistakes will start to appear as the limit of his capacity is approached; when capacity is exceeded, total breakdown may occur. It is not difficult to see why this should be so. To say that capacity has been reached is to say that all the recipient's psychic resources have been mobilized to deal with input. The knowledge that error has occurred is itself a deflection of some part of these resources, and, unless the subject can be trained to disregard such knowledge and its disturbing after-effects, the stage for disintegration will be set. We may expect to find a narrow zone just short of the subject's capacity where mistakes will start to occur and where his behaviour will approximate to that of a man-made system when noise is producing a mild loss, but a point will soon be reached where he will cease to behave in anyway usefully. The practical implication is clear; tasks that call for the continuous processing of simple information must be designed so that their demands fall well within the operator's capacity.

The human subject always tends to impose meaning on material (cf. Bartlett's effort after meaning), and this tendency acts so as to extend the amount of material he can handle. If we try to recall a string of digits, we automatically resort to groupings and rhythmical effects; if the presentation is visual, the tendency asserts itself in attempts at patterning.

With content information the human listener tries with varying success to compensate for loss by extrapolating from the cues he picks up. In this sense it is possible for a recipient to add (sometimes incorrectly) to the information he receives; no such addition can, of course, occur in an artificial system. The extent to which such compensation can be made cannot be expressed quantitatively, since its possibility is dependent on the listener's store of background information which varies from subject to subject. In addition, successful extrapolation depends on the receiver's level of intelligence. Sometimes the hearing of a single word or phrase can throw light on wide areas that were formerly in darkness. In this way an intelligent person can retrieve large quantities of information which he has allowed to slip past him; a similar mechanism can be brought to bear in skimming the cream from a text. The basis of this possibility lies in the fact that all content information entails some degree of redundancy; a sentence is not a succession of words in the sense that a number is a succession of digits. If the meaning of a sentence is thought of as a unique object to be discriminated from a host of other possible objects, we can see that as a sentence (or any larger unit) progresses, the number of possible meanings is reduced, until, if all goes well, the hearer or reader is left with the meaning intended. Admittedly this is a highly artificial way of regarding the reading process, but information theory was not designed for such occasions. Our justification for applying the model in this sort of context is that it throws light on certain features of the process.

The intake of information by the human being can be studied at the level of the single pulse of attention and at that of continuing reception (which can be regarded as a succession of pulses). Linkage between pulses is effected through short-term memory; retention, recall and recognition are dependent on the integration of new content into the existing system of long-term memory. The interaction of long-term and short-term memory in the processing of information has been investigated in a series of recent experiments by Glanzer (39), whose work in this field will be discussed in more detail in Part 4. Limitation failures of communication occur most simply where the input of sign information exceeds the capacity of the single pulse. The intake of continuous content information depends both on pulse capacity and on the quality of interpretation made possible by long-term memory.

'I cannot keep up with this speed' implies a simpler type of failure than 'He went so fast I couldn't see what he was getting at.' In the first instance there is no possibility of retrieval after two or three seconds, since the elements lost bear no relation to those retained; in the second an illuminating phrase or display sometimes affords a chance of retrieval later.

A man who is proficient at one level of understanding is not always successful in attaining the next. There are, for example, many who can observe and make rational inferences in a practical situation but who cannot operate at the level of general ideas. This is a fairly clear instance of cognitive limitation. More complex is the case of the person who, while effective in dealing with instances that conform to a known rule, is at sea the moment an exceptional case arises. Here we cannot be sure whether the limitation occurs in the field of cognition or that of personality or both. This distinction has something in common with that between the routine worker and the man able to fill a managerial role. Higher up the scale is the political leader who thinks with effectiveness at the level to which he is habituated, but is unable to adapt when events are translated to a higher plane. English history saw illustrations of this in two Prime Ministers of the thirties, Baldwin who is credited with handling a domestic affair like an abdication with skill but who failed to evaluate the threat of Hitler, and Chamberlain who, replacing Baldwin's inertia with his own brisk decisiveness, was no more successful at estimating the German threat realistically. The man who suffers from this sort of limitation does not as a rule break down; on the contrary, his failure to rise to the level of events leads him to treat the new as though it were familiar, the highly complex as the ordinarily complicated. Churchill, in another context, remarked: 'When there is a flood, the habits of the four-inch conduit do not change. It continues to transmit its customary flow, cheerfully rejecting the rest.'

17 Distraction

Lyubov   Thank you, Firs, thank you, dear old man,
           I'm so glad to find you still alive.
Firs   The day before yesterday.
Gaev   He's rather deaf.

The Cherry Orchard, Act I

Under the rubric of distraction may be included all the re-
maining extraneous factors that interfere with the reception of
messages. By extraneous is meant unrelated to meaning or interpretation; that is, this type of factor will impede reception, irrespective of the message's content. It operates without regard to the
receiver's state of information, his attitudes and orientations,
and in its extremer forms it can prevent the reception of the
simplest and clearest message.

There are four main types of distractor:

1) The competing stimulus.
2) Environmental stress.
3) Subjective stress.
4) Ignorance of the medium.

Only the first—and just possibly the second—qualify as distractors in the generally accepted sense. The point that links the
four in the present context is that all detract from good reception
in an undiscriminating way.

The competing stimulus

The closest parallel to the noise of artificial systems is interference
by unwanted stimuli in the same modality as the communication.
The most disruptive form of this will be the stimulus that bears
the closest affinity to the signal, e.g. a bogus blip near the blip
that is being tracked, a conversation on the same theme as the one

the receiver is trying to follow. Extreme irrelevance is comparatively easy to disregard, unless it occurs in an extreme way—a blinding flash, a thunderous roar, an outrageous social solecism, all of which disrupt by shock rather than by intellectual confusion. Introspection cannot be trusted to reveal the degrees of disruption various types of interference bring about; the effects of each sort of undesired stimulus must be experimentally determined.

Environmental stress

What we think of as the ideal conditions for receiving communication (i.e. those that promote reasonable physical and mental relaxation) can be resolved into a number of environmental states to which levels of adaptation have been established. If one or more of these conditions becomes greatly exaggerated, it will end by affecting behaviour, including that of attending to a message. The more important of these conditions are temperature, humidity, ventilation, vibration, noise and glare. Again it is dangerous to base estimates of such effects on subjective impression, partly because annoyance and discomfort do not necessarily correlate with decrement of performance. Up to a point performance can be maintained in the face of such irritants, at other times it declines without any consciousness of discomfort. Similarly, the extent to which different conditions reinforce each other must be studied experimentally. There is evidence that the same mechanisms are brought into play by some conditions but not by others. There are also considerable individual differences in response to these conditions, what is barely noticeable change to one man causing acute discomfort to another.

Internal stress

Here we are thinking of such things as sleeplessness, ill-health, the effects of drugs, sensory deprivation and mood variations. Some of these make us conscious of great difficulty in attending to incoming messages, others lead to exaggeration of success in interpreting them. Transient conditions present different problems from permanent ones (e.g. total blindness) and those that exert a gradually increasing grip (e.g. failures in sight and hearing).

These in turn differ from one another, the person with a growing defect being able to call on past experiences stored in long-term memory, a factor which sets his problems apart from those who have never known the use of some channel of communication.

Ignorance of the communicating medium

We find a fourth type of distraction where two people are prevented from an exchange of experience by the absence of a medium with which both are familiar. This occurs primarily when the medium is linguistic and can take a one-way or two-way form; there can be many degrees of ignorance in either, e.g. the student listening to a lecturer in another tongue, the authorities from two countries battling to discuss a topic of common interest.

The parties to any of these distractor situations may or may not be of the same intellectual level or possess the same background information. Whether they are or not is irrelevant; the factor that binds the situations under the same standard is unrelated to message content or mental ability.

18 The unstated assumption

'Sir Keith Joseph, Minister of Housing and Local Government, pointed out that in an earlier debate on the Bill *Hansard* reported him as saying that any Housing Minister was "honestly wicked" while a shortage remained.

'What he actually said was: "Any Housing Minister is on a sticky wicket while a shortage remains."'

Daily Telegraph, 14 April 1964

The commonest source of everyday misunderstanding originates in the speaker or writer making an assumption which he thinks it unnecessary to render explicit. The assumption may concern the meaning of a single word or phrase, the information implicit in a proposition, or acquaintance with a whole area of discussion. This barrier is essentially of a cognitive character, that is to say, failure is due to ignorance or lack of information on the receiver's part, not in his predisposition to interpret what is said in terms of his own mental sets—failures of the latter sort spring from more complex sources.

Cross-purpose talking may develop over the use of proper names. A lot of information can be dissipated before it dawns on either party that the speaker's Fred or Jones is someone other than the listener's. The fault usually lies with the speaker, who assumes that a name which has unique application in his repertory has the same restricted use in the recipient's.

Ambiguities over single words or phrases can occur at many levels of sophistication. One of the crudest derives from the mishearing of formalized utterances ('Three chairs for the Headmaster', 'Our father Richard in heaven'). The assumption here is that repetition makes explanation superfluous. The solecisms of travellers are traceable sometimes to a misreading of the dictionary, at others to confusion between similar sounding words. (*Je désire deux matelots*: English lady ordering twin beds.)

Subtler and less easily detectable are peripheral variations in the connotations of general terms. Here the problem is that the variations are seldom gross enough to force the lack of full agreement into the open. The use of the same words to signify approximately the same things engenders a false belief in the objectivity of statements and opinions. Recognition of this was one of the main factors leading to the birth of deductive reasoning in the time of Socrates and Plato. This recognition led to a mistrust of language as a medium for the expression of opinion derived from daily experience. Against this, these thinkers sought to install knowledge arrived at by disciplined reasoning. Observation and experiment as methods of sifting and extracting the elements of concrete experience had yet to be developed.

Anyone who tries to communicate ideas must be aware of the need to grope for appropriate words and phrases to express them. The tools of language are not arranged in neat systems ready to be taken down to fit the next occasion. This is an admission that we are forced to adapt and extend the use of words whenever we go beyond the repetition of catch phrases and ready-made opinions. Thus we must be alert to the inevitability of shifting meanings and to the need to draw attention to any slant we are giving to important terms.

A variant of the single-word assumption can occur when the speaker projects awareness of his own environment on to a recipient whose viewpoint may be quite different. Something of the sort appears to have led to the charge of the Light Brigade at Balaclava, when the Commander-in-Chief sent a message by runner ordering an attack on the enemy, the enemy visible to him being a small isolated detachment. The recipient could only interpret the message in terms of the main Russian army deployed in full array before him.

Usually confusion over a single word passes unnoticed; B interprets the message in his own way without suspecting that anything has gone astray. The situation arising from an unstated *proposition* is more likely to give rise to bafflement, and the recipient gets the uncomfortable feeling that he is not extracting the full meaning of what he hears. It may appear that the remedy lies in his own hands; he should say, 'Before we go any further, there is something I'm not clear about.' Obvious though such a course may seem, it is not always easy to follow it. Many listeners, for example, will start by assuming that the fault is in themselves and can be put right through a reinforcement of attention. Sometimes this works out satisfactorily, and we are made thankful we did not draw comment on ourselves needlessly. There is at other times the fear that interruption will disturb the social context, that the man who appears to be commanding an audience will be deflected from his purpose, the sole outcome of the questioner's enterprise being to disrupt an agreeable occasion. More serious than either of these difficulties is that of ascertaining what the source of one's perplexity is and so of deciding what question to ask. This dilemma is met when the speaker is using familiar terms, but in spite of this his argument is felt to be taking an oblique course. It is as though the listener is unable to orient himself, as if there has been a transposition of objects in a well-known scene. When such a situation is analysed, it is often found that there has been some adjustment of the main reference points and that information about this is missing. Fifteen years ago the writer when visiting India was told of the difficulty the authorities were experiencing in adopting Hindi as the official language. The decision to make this change had been taken and could not be reversed; the trouble was that Hindi was a tongue understood by only a negligible proportion of the population, whereas Hindustani—a hybrid based on Hindi, Urdu and English—was widely understood so that its adoption would have presented no problem. A year later he visited India again and was surprised to be told that Hindi was now in general use. What nobody pointed out was that tacit agreement had been reached to substitute the word 'Hindi' for 'Hindustani'.

As ignorance of an unstated assumption can lead to confusion of thought, ignorance about a conclusion or decision sometimes results in confused activity. A famous Cabinet meeting early in the First World War ended with Churchill under the impression that a campaign in the Dardanelles had been agreed on, while Kitchener believed that it had been rejected. The outcome of this misunderstanding was a half-baked adventure which did untold harm to the Allied cause.

The educational world is an arena in which the unstated assumption can play havoc through ineffective presentation, discontinuity of instruction, or the broken attendance of individual pupils. The foundation of many life-long obstacles to the grasp of different school subjects has undoubtedly been laid through early failure to come to terms with some basic definition or explanation. It is to be hoped that current methods, particularly in reading, writing and computation, will in future do much to avoid the formation of indestructible resistances. The linear programme with its painless progressions is one of several techniques devised to this end.

In everyday intercourse a great deal depends on the communicator's perceptiveness. Inability to gauge the other person's state of information may spring from several causes. The speaker may forget that the terms he finds it natural to use have been acquired as the result of long training and study; he may fear to bore his hearer with what is mistakenly felt to be obvious; or he may try to say too much and perhaps be too lazy to bother with preliminary explanations. A subtler fault arises from difficulty in assessing the amount of redundant statement needed. To assess this accurately calls for awareness of the recipient's stock of associations; some speakers lack this type of perceptiveness almost completely, while the sensitive talker is continuously alert to the effects his words are producing—it is as though he receives unspoken messages from his audience which convert what is formally a one-way communication into a kind of two-way flow.

The inexperienced writer is at times guilty of withholding vital information from his reader. Those producing their first scientific papers frequently make the mistake of assuming that what is obvious to them (e.g. the purpose of their research) must be self evident. They therefore wade into complexities of detail without giving clear indication of the course they are meaning to set. A related weakness is the belief that the bare mention of a point, irrespective of the position and emphasis assigned to it, provides adequate coverage. This is, of course, not true. It is part of any writer's task to ensure that whatever needs to be said registers with the proper weight.

It may be that the difficulty experienced by some physical scientists in accepting psychology as a scientific discipline is rooted in an unrecognized assumption. Experiments in physics and chemistry lead generally to results in which a very high level of confidence can be placed, or, more accurately, only results of such an order are likely to hold much of interest in these contexts. In psychology, such high levels are attained comparatively rarely, but prediction at more modest levels can be of great practical value. One reason for this lies in the plasticity of human behaviour, which implies that behavioural prediction is usually set within comparatively wide limits rather than at a single point. The physical scientist, reasoning from his own experience in the laboratory, may interpret this tolerance as vague and woolly, and perhaps make the inference that it is the outcome of a sloppy experimental technique. Most psychologists would argue that it requires scrupulous technique to attain a barely perceptible level of significant prediction.

It would be easy to multiply instances of the confusions attributable to the unstated assumption. Here are two to which attention was drawn in the same recent television programme: (a) European music is customarily developed along a single rhythmical line, so that the European listener assumes that all music is likely to be uni-rhythmical. As long as he makes this assumption he will get little satisfaction from most African music, which frequently deploys four or five rhythms simultaneously. (b) A painting traditionally presents a theme (not necessarily in representative terms) realized objectively in a two-dimensional composition. Some contemporary painting does not set out with this intention; it is rather an exploration in paint, a commentary on a process undergone by the artist, and attempts to assess it in the accepted terms are likely to be unavailing. Whether it is possible to communicate this kind of an exploration and whether artists with these intentions are interested in making communications are separate matters.

Finally we must not assume that the sole purpose of communication is to ensure full understanding by every hearer. Such an ideal would entail the banishment of wit and vivacity from human discourse and the anaesthetization of keener intellects by laborious explanation. In these matters the speaker must at times take calculated risks; sometimes his remarks will fall on stony ground and he will have lost the gamble.

19 Incompatibility of schemas

THE three sources of communication failure so far discussed are easy to grasp at the level of daily occurrence. No one would dispute that there are limits to the speed with which the human being can accept information, that his reception is interfered with by external and internal distractors, or that it can be bewildering to have to pick up the threads of a narrative or argument if we are uncertain of its point of departure. Behind each of these broad observations lies a host of problems that only the trained investigator is likely to recognize, but the phenomena themselves are familiar to everyone capable of rudimentary reflection.

The next obstacle is of a less obvious kind. It is not on the face of it clear why the same information should mean widely different things to different people, and while disputes, often of the bitterest kind, are known to occur over such things, it is usually felt that a little patience and tolerance should enable us to avoid them. This is an over-simplification which fails to take account of three fundamental issues. The first of these is that the receiving of information entails far more interpretation than most people are aware of; the second concerns the means by which interpretation is brought about; the third the extent to which these means vary from one person to another, or even within the same individual at different stages of his life. It is the third of these which has directest relevance to the problems of communication, but to discuss it with any hope of making headway it will be necessary to start with a few words about the others.

'No information without interpretation' is implicit in the statement that perception represents a transaction between the human subject and his environment. It is a repudiation of the passivity view; the view of mind as an uncritical reflector enunciated three centuries ago by John Locke, echoed by many associationists and atomists, and implicit in the approach of the earliest (and crudest) behaviourists. Few if any contemporary psychologists would give it unqualified acceptance, though that is no proof that it may not exert an unacknowledged influence on their thinking. Many of the earliest findings of experimental psychology (Weber's Law, for example) made nonsense of the passivity hypothesis, but it was left to the gestaltists to throw down the gauntlet. No one could observe a phenomenon, where the successive flashing of separated points of light gives rise to an illusion of movement between them, and maintain the existence of perfect correlation between the elements of stimulus and response. From the point of view of communication, the essential feature is that the human being is selective in his responses, that he is seldom aware of his selectiveness, and that in consequence his day-to-day experiences give him an unduly simple account of his relationship to the external world. However often he is told that his nervous system is to be regarded as a network of related media linking him with his environment, he cannot rid himself of the illusion that he experiences the environment directly, 'as it really is'.

If human beings recorded their surroundings mechanically, their perceptions would be independent of maturation or learning and so of long-term memory. They might perhaps store past impressions, but their present impressions would not be influenced by the contents of that store. There is, however, compelling evidence of a dynamic element in perception and the more complex forms of mental activity, however much inertia and habit are apt to obscure it. Thus we are bound to ask how new information becomes related to old, and how past experience predisposes an organism to behave in certain ways rather than in others. What is actually known about the factors that establish continuity in the individual's experience? In some ways little enough, but experiment has put it beyond doubt that such continuity exists and conceptual thought has gone some way to ordering our notions about what happens. Our first need is to find a label for those sets and attitudes that affect our reception of new information; the term most likely to assist is schema. This is a descriptive rather than an operational concept, and in adopting it as an aid in the present context we may find ourselves extending its application even further than many of its users have done.

The history of the word schema is well known to psychologists and can be touched on very briefly. It was used first by Stout and was adopted by Head in 1920 'to explain how changes in the posture of a part of the body are recognized'. From this Head developed the notion of the body-image as a state of awareness intermediate between the body and the environment it is set in. It is essential for the concept to be understood dynamically; the body, especially in a growing creature, is not a static mass, and its image, if it is to serve its purpose effectively, must reflect its expansions and shrinkages. Bartlett twelve years later generalized this psycho-physiological concept so as to cover any 'active organization of past reactions or of past experiences which must always be supposed to be operating in any well-adapted organic response'. Twenty years ago Oldfield and Zangwill (81) examined the history of the concept in a series of articles entitled 'Head's concept of the schema and its application in contemporary British psychology'. About the same time Wolters in a paper, 'Some biological aspects of thinking', stressed that schematic organizations are essentially 'living and flexible'.

More recently M. D. Vernon (102, 103) has described schemas as 'persistent, deep-rooted and well-organized classifications of ways of perceiving, thinking and behaving', and Meredith (75) has referred to them as 'more or less enduring patterns of brain activity resulting from an abstraction made by the individual in response to some important feature in his experience'. Meredith has elaborated this definition by enumerating five characteristics. First, the schema is modified by learning; if it were not, it would have little value for practical living. If, for example, a grown man retained the body-image of a child, he would be endlessly damaging himself. Secondly, the schema is functional; its purpose is to supply us with an inner working model of some aspect of the world. Thirdly, each schema must be thought of as possessing its own life and energy, and of reaching out and influencing other schemas. Fourthly, the schemas in one man's mind will be related in some kind of hierarchy, with the body-image in the role of proto-schema. Finally, the diversity of the nervous system is likely to be reflected in the diversity of schemas, the latter representing abstractions made by the senses from the energy impinging on our systems from the environment. Hence there will be schemas relating to the different qualities of experience, colour schemas, sound schemas, schemas for taste, smell, touch and movement, schemas of shape and pattern, of space and time; value schemas, location schemas, schemas representing scientific and cultural ways of thinking. Thus 'what we call the "mind" of the individual is a schematic adjustive system. It consists of economical abstractions from experience made partly by the individual and partly by the race, which work together in a more or less systematic fashion to enable the individual to make that ever-necessary series of adjustments which we call "living".'

The schema also plays an essential role in Piaget's account of intellectual development. The nature of this role has been described by Lovell (69):

> 'The process of adapting to the environment and organizing experience results in experiences of physical or mental actions which have definite structure, called schemas, which in turn become the tools for handling further encounters with the environment. It is in the growth of these intellectual structures that Piaget has been particularly interested . . . Once new experience is assimilated, the child's schemas are more complex, and, because of this, more complex accommodations are possible. Moreover, in Piaget's view, the child's schemas do not remain unchanged even in the absence of environmental stimulation, for meanings are constantly reorganized, and linked with other meanings.'

So far the schema has been considered primarily in cognitive terms. We make systematic selections from recurrent experience which offer us a way of looking at and dealing with the world. Some of these have a collective, others an individual source. It is to be expected that individuals will tend to share the first and to differ in regard to the second. But abstractions are not made only in cognitive matters; they occur also in the affective field and it seems justifiable, at least for our present purpose, to apply the word schema in this direction also. Human beings make abstractions from their experience not merely in terms of the qualities of external objects but also of their feelings and reactions. Their tendency to do this has been studied by many workers with an interest in personality traits and types, and on the face of it many of these classifications share the characteristics of the schema. Thus it is the aim of projective tests to study the basis of affective selectivity as revealed through the responses of different individuals to emotionally ambiguous material. Jung, Kretschmer, Murray, Allport and a host of other investigators have been concerned to lay bare the main dimensions of selectivity and have shown that the same data elicit from one subject evidence of a bias to achievement, from a second to resentment, from a third to sociability. It seems, then, that if we are to get a full picture of an individual's outlook and so of the communications he is likely to make and the interpretations he will put upon those he receives, we must take into account all the schemas he has evolved in both the cognitive and affective domains. In brief, people approach life with varying expectations and reaction patterns, which lead them to build contrasted pictures of the environment and to interpret phenomena accordingly. These influences operate at every level, biochemical, neural, perceptual, conceptual and attitudinal.

Earlier we spoke of perceptions and concepts as the main units of cognition, and of attitudes as the main units of the affective life. We are now reaching the position that all of these share the characteristics of schemas; they do so at least to the extent that they continue to assimilate fresh content. We should note, however, that cognitive schemas tend to have an objective orientation, whereas affective schemas are necessarily related to the subject's preferences and aversions. This means that the first are likely to be modified in response to environmental change, while the second will bend the environment to their own image. This suggests that where the schemas of two persons are incompatible, the affective sort are likely to offer the greater barriers to communication.

At this point it may help to consider the individual in relation to one or two representative schemas. The function of the body-image is to help the subject to relate himself physically to his environment, including the people he meets. It is fairly obvious that the body-image will, among other things, supply a standard of comparison in such matters as height and size. Hence the individual's interpretation of tall and short will be influenced by self-perception. In other words, his interpretation of terms like big and little, fat and thin, old and young are likely to be subjectively coloured. It is true that he will also be aware of more objective definitions; e.g. whatever his own height or age, he will know that men over six feet are considered tall and people over seventy old. We may expect, then, that the applications of general terms of this sort will be affected by two norms, a personal norm—whoever is taller than me is tall—and an impersonal one—the average man is so high. This warns us that we must expect disparate interpretations of many terms that at first sight appear to have an exclusively objective reference.

Before we attempt to present the chief types of incompatibility, it will be of interest to look at the ways in which schemas can be consciously planted and cultivated. So far we have spoken of them as more or less spontaneous reactions to the environment, involving the subject in no initial choice. There are, however, situations where the human being deliberately sets up a schema to serve a specific purpose. The three examples we shall give are drawn from the worlds of music, science and education.

One of the most firmly established styles of musical composition is the theme and variations. In this the composer selects or invents a theme with the intention of developing a series of pieces in each of which the opening statement can be recognized. The point in common between the schema and the musical theme is that each supplies a common denominator to a wide range of particular happenings. It will perhaps throw light on the properties of a good schema if we consider what a musician regards as essential to a suitable theme. Stanford (94) in *Musical Composition* names three important attributes: the theme must contain sufficient material to vary; it must possess at least one striking feature; and it must be simple. Of the first essential he says, 'Abundance of suggestive material is a self-evident necessity. If there is not enough contrast in the phrases, the writer will run dry of ideas for the variations. But they should be only suggestions, which the variations may be left to elaborate.' When he speaks of a striking feature, he is thinking of such things as dynamic contrast and an unusual rhythm, and by simplicity he is pointing at a basic and easily recognized unity. It can be argued that these three attributes, divested of their musical trappings, qualify all general concepts. In other words, a concept's survival value depends on its unity, its specificity and its capacity to be invested in a wide variety of particular occasions. Of these the last attribute is the most important—for music and for psychology. The ability to discriminate themes and ideas containing the seeds of development from those that are self-contained is among the most highly valued in all cultural activity.

When investigating any set of phenomena, the scientist starts by seeking for a working model which appears capable of containing them. He says in effect, 'Things appear to work in this way' and, having satisfied himself that his explanation contains no obvious weakness, he converts it into the question, 'Do things in fact work like this?' If the hypothesis is verified by experiment, he is likely to press forward with a further question, 'Is my model specific to this set of happenings, or can it be extended to cover other sets?' The more comprehensive the model is found to be, the more basic the research; the highest achievements of scientific insight lie in the formulation of models that explain many sets of apparently dissimilar circumstances. Rather as a fertile musical theme lends itself to innumerable developments without losing its identity, a fertile scientific model is found to have applications that were not specified in its initial formulation.

Here we should remind ourselves that we began by defining a schema as an enduring pattern of brain activity, and we must be careful not to press the analogy between schemas and models too closely. A musical theme is a set of notes, a scientific model is a statement about how phenomena are related; we may infer that these set up patterns of brain activity, but we must remember that these patterns have not been actually observed. We can observe notes, explanations and the words used to describe general ideas and concepts, and we observe that the most useful of these help us to link new and old experiences. When we ask how this is possible, we feel forced to say that our brain and nervous systems have been modified in some lasting way, and we call these inferred modifications schemas.

The educator aims to set up ways of perceiving and thinking that will enable the developing mind to assimilate more and more material. It is a truism to say that good teaching methods are successful in this respect and that poor methods fail. In terms of the present argument we may say that what the good teacher does is to plant and tend the growth of valuable schemas in the minds of his pupils. Rote learning (though at times necessary) and the teaching of school subjects in isolation from one another appear unlikely to do this. Controlled experiments have been conducted to test the effectiveness of different schematic approaches to the learning of the same material, the purpose being to determine the characteristics in each type of schema that favour and retard learning. This amounts to an attempt to place one type of schema on an operational footing. If we can predict, as Skemp has attempted to do (93), that children taught by approach A will learn and retain material more effectively than those taught by approach B, we are on the way to converting the schema from a descriptive to an experimental concept. One obvious instance of this lies in the Pitman alphabet, by which the young children of at least 1,500 schools are today being taught to read. If the claims of its originators are substantiated (or even perhaps if they are not), our knowledge of practical learning theory will have been enhanced.

The point we have been leading up to is that objects and events are experienced through the medium of schemas and that people with radically different schemas will assimilate and interpret data in different ways. Their descriptions of the same data will at times vary to the point of being unrecognizable. We have seen that there are schemas of such generality that in a sense everyone may be said to share them, and also that there are schemas of a specific kind. We must now consider first how schemas of the general sort can give rise to discrepant information and then how accounts of the same objects can vary through the adoption of incompatible schemas.

The body-image is a schema of a general sort in the sense that everybody develops one, specific in that no two body schemas will be identical. Apart from lack of identity, the development of such schemas is likely to vary in other ways, e.g. one man's will reflect the position of his limbs more accurately than another's, the man who uses his hands in a skilled way will acquire high sensitivity in respect of them, while one who lacks specific skills may be expected to have an image lacking in localized specialization. High-diving instructors say that champions of this art possess instantaneous awareness of the position of every limb; this knowledge prompts all manner of minor corrections in fractional time and so leads to perfection of style. Doubtless, a similar sort of awareness characterizes psychomotor skill of every kind; whether its medium is visual or kinaesthetic imagery is not fully known, though one would expect the latter to play at least a major part. The late Matthias Alexander ascribed many of civilized man's ailments to faulty posture induced through defective body-imagery; indeed the goal of his teaching might be described as re-education in this field of self-perception. Faults of this type seem likely to result from inaccurate or unduly delayed feedback of information, shortcomings that can mar the transmission of any physiological data. It may be that a similar inertia hampers the effectiveness of the more psychological kind of message; most people would probably admit a tendency to brush aside new data which called for amendment to existing ideas.

Schemas may be termed incompatible when they present irreconcilable accounts of the same data. We do not have to look far for examples: the same dream interpreted by Freud, Jung or Adler; the same neurotic symptom viewed by a behaviour therapist and an interview therapist; the same piece of goal-seeking activity seen through the eyes of Skinner and McClelland. How deep do these differences go? To take a balanced view of these discrepancies, it should first be appreciated that no investigator can pursue every hypothesis that occurs to him. The one he elects to follow may not in the beginning appear to be superior to the ones he rejects, but time may associate his name with the first and the others with those of rivals. Where this happens it is possible for both parties to take a detached attitude, as though they have adopted conflicting roles as a convenient division of labour.

It would, however, be mistaken to assume that all professional rivalries are of this sort. Even in science, there are some who cannot escape the toils of identification and involvement, and it must be conceded that these conditions seem sometimes to impart a dynamism not always apparent in the efforts of the more objective. Some perhaps would be lost without the courage of their distortions. Whether those who attain this frame of mind are truly unable to see other viewpoints or whether they cannot afford to admit as much is a question beyond this inquiry. What is relevant is that in all walks of life we find people, often of high intelligence, who behave as though certain lines of explanation are not merely wrong but unimaginable. To account for this, we must postulate ways of thinking and feeling that are unable to coexist.

A few pages back it was noted that the abstractions which give rise to schemas are made partly by the individual and partly by the race. It seems justifiable to extrapolate between these extremes by interjecting small-group schemas (family, school, club) and large-group schemas (nation, sex, age-group). The totality of schemas making up the individual's psychic armoury will be drawn from all these sources.

There is one question that is unlikely to be fully answered for a long time to come. This concerns the origin of schemas, why some schemas come to be developed rather than others. Where they are consciously evolved, subjected to empirical trials and the best selected for future use, no problem arises, but it is not always easy to see that those adopted less deliberately have survived a similar testing. To what extent are those adopted by the individual dependent on neurological, biochemical, endocrinological or psychological factors? How far are they fostered by his early environment, and how far are they a reaction against it? How far are they the result of conditioning, how far of heredity? How permanent are they, how easily destroyed? Similarly with the schemas of large groups. It was said earlier that each language has evolved through its own selection of phonemes which became organized into its particular sound system. Also, that a language elaborates its own syntactical structure, the contrast between the structures of any two languages exerting an effect on the communications each can make, so that it is sometimes impossible to translate adequately from one tongue to another. When we encounter this, we are apt to speak, say, of characteristically French and English modes of expression. But a phrase like this begs many important questions.

In spite of all that remains unsolved in this complex area, one or two positive statements can be made. We can see, for example, why schemas are a necessity for thinking and communicating, and we can see at least two reasons why they should vary from person to person. Without schemas there would be no continuity or development in individual experience and no possibility of communication between one human being and another. Living would be a moment-to-moment affair; there would be no social groups, merely aggregations of psychopathic individuals, each dominated by the impressions of the moment. Variation in the development of schemas can be expected first because it is the function of many of them to relate the individual to his environment, secondly because his capacity for handling information is so small compared to the amount that assails him; this forces him to devise principles of selection, and there is no obvious reason why all human beings should adopt identical principles. Men are known both by observation and experiment to differ in respect of abilities, modes of imagery, types of reaction, physique, tastes, personality, appearance and strength of need, and it is to be expected that these variations should be related to their ways of interpreting the outside world.

A problem of particular interest concerns the values and attitudes of different generations. The organic changes that occur throughout life predispose us to think that young and old will view many things differently. Such differences may be exaggerated or underestimated, but nobody has thought it sensible to suggest that they do not exist. What is hard is to determine how far these perennial shiftings are overlaid by changes in the climate of opinion. This theme should prove a challenge to the social psychologist; indeed, at least one research bearing on it has been conducted in this country. This was Kelvin's (61) attempt to find out through the readers of *New Society* the views of different age-groups on the factors that had made England a great nation in the past and those that were likely to make for greatness in the future. Admittedly the sample was biased in that it was drawn mainly from readers of one journal, but this did not lead to any obvious uniformity of view. One of the things suggested by the tables was that the 20–40 groups (roughly those born between 1923 and 1943) tended to an extreme radicalism in the main areas (defence, immigration laws, education, sex), whereas the under 20s and the 40s–60s to some extent shared a more traditional approach. What this valuable piece of work could not unravel was how far such a pattern might have been discerned among the generations of any period and how far it is the product of our recent history.

20 Influence of unconscious and partly conscious mechanisms

'Fear is an affect of great potency in determining what the individual will perceive, think and do. Fear is the most constricting of all the affects. It can result in perceiving what is characterized as "tunnel vision", where the victim becomes functionally blind to a large proportion of the potential perceptual field. It can produce thinking that is slow, narrow in scope, and rigid in form. It brings about a tensing and tightening of muscles and other motor apparatuses, and in terror a "frozen", immobile body. Fear greatly reduces behavioural alternatives.'

Carroll E. Izard and Silvan S. Tomkins (57)

It is not only fear that creates its own world of perception; similar statements could be written of each of the main affects, whether positive or negative. The chief mechanisms responsible for these selections and distortions are the same at least for the negative affects. Freud, one of the earliest expositors in this field, laid particular emphasis on the concepts of projection, repression and identification, and, while Freudian theory is accepted less uncritically than thirty years ago, there are few who would be ready to jettison these terms completely.

Projection is said to occur when the subject interprets the behaviour of another in terms of his own unconscious needs and impulses; it is the function of the projective test to lay bare the direction of these needs. It is claimed that the material used in such tests evokes one pattern of response from some people and different patterns from others, and that these patterns are consistently related to the outlook and personality of the individual respondent. If this is true, it illustrates in a concise way that the recipient of information is prone to slant his interpretation in accordance with his desires and fears; in brief, that interpretation plays a far bigger role in the receipt of information than is usually recognized.*

Identification is closely related to projection; when we project our motives on to another's behaviour, we identify that person with ourself. There are, however, occasions when it is customary to stress the identification element, e.g. if a person sides vehemently with a character in a play or a novel, he is said to be identified with that character or his situation. When the same thing occurs in real life, it is probable that the subject will reject information inconsistent with the case to which he feels committed.

Repression can lead to the full rejection of unwelcome information. The subject will behave as if he has not seen or heard material too painful to admit to consciousness or incompatible with some strongly held belief. These mechanisms operate at the level of everyday normality, as when fears or expectations lead us to make false inferences about matters in which we feel involved. At a deeper and more systematic level they distort the outlook of the mentally disturbed, notably in paranoia, where all roads lead to persecution, and in melancholia with its burdens of guilt.

It would, however, be shallow to ascribe all difficulty in making contact with the mentally ill to confusion in the latter's attempts at communication. There are times when the experiences of the sick person lead him to speak with a clarity and simplicity which threaten the complacency of the healthy. It requires concentration and candour to receive such pronouncements adequately, and failure to do this enhances the sufferer's sense of isolation. In general, the healthy will admit the existence of pain and injustice, but this calls for nugatory effort compared with submission to the poignant story of the individual victim. For this reason the torments of many patients remain unshared and the cries of the abandoned unheard.

Three very different types of phenomena remain to be indicated under this chapter's heading. First, the social taboo. Every society has its approved and embargoed values, the sum of which goes

---

* It would be mistaken to limit the application of the projection concept to a psychiatric context. The first attempts to account for some aspects of the external world usually contain a projective element, the observer seeking to explain the behaviour of objects in terms of his own processes. Thus early notions of force and causation are impregnated with suggestions derived from our own experience of muscular effort and volition.

far to defining its climate of opinion. The formation of this climate supplies a theme of great intricacy, as does the manner in which it changes and the way these changes communicate themselves. The theme assumes particular complexity in a liberal society intolerant of past taboos and the open suppression of opinion. While it is a great thing to have outgrown ruthless persecution, it is dangerous to assume that in doing so all the problems of free expression have been solved. Rack and stake are not the only instruments that can control opinion (not that they were always successful); the smear and the slant can be equally telling and are harder to detect. Whereas the taboos of former times operated through overt veto, those of today assert themselves through suggestion and hidden persuasion.

This last phrase has been popularized by the American publicist, Vance Packard (84), in quite another context. Packard has been concerned at the exploitation of motivational research in the formation and control of purchaser attitudes. These activities began innocuously enough in the commercial field. Where several lines of a product are virtually indistinguishable in content, the manufacturer is advised how to outstrip his rivals in the presentation of his own line. The firm which appeals most successfully through the creation of a flattering consumer-image is likely to reach a corresponding reward in profits. In addition, the needs of America's expanding economy have set the pace for continual impulse purchasing, the revival of interest in goods long considered to be without appeal and of habits that encourage the citizen to renew his buying of staple goods at ever shorter intervals. It is hard to draw the line between the harmless and the offensive, but any responsible psychologist must be alive to the dangers of systematic depth probing, whether the object to be sold is a toothpaste or a politician. An instrument forged to control the sale of merchandise can lend itself to more sinister transactions.

Paranormal cognition still constitutes a vexed area of research. Though some deny the existence of evidence for telepathy and clairvoyance, others take such phenomena for granted, while agreeing that their mechanisms are not understood. From the standpoint of communication, such matters raise special difficulties, because—their incidence being sporadic—no observer can be convinced by an appeal to direct experience; one man can invite another to share the experiences of sight and hearing, but, in the western world at least, extra-sensory phenomena have eluded almost all efforts to bring them under experimental control. Those who claim to have experienced such things seem to accept them as private happenings whose existence is beyond question; but because their authenticity cannot be verified by appeal to any other sense, many questions concerning them remain virtually unasked. Scientific education, with its emphasis on empirical data and precise observation, has developed a strong resistance to phenomena that cannot be accounted for in its customary terms. This resistance is justified in so far as a high proportion of the accounts of allegedly abnormal events can be traced to slovenly thinking and faulty observation. But there are times when the trained scientist is guilty of equally glaring defects. Not long ago an able physiologist (not of this country) was demonstrating the uses of a decompression chamber and explaining how the performance of subjects engaged on cognitive tasks suffered almost instantaneous collapse if a sharp change of pressure was introduced. Asked if there was any way of resisting such changes, he answered, 'No way at all. The only person who has ever done such a thing was a Yogi who continued his arithmetic as though nothing had happened.' Pressed to account for the Yogi's apparent immunity, the demonstrator conveyed that he neither knew nor cared how it had been achieved, implying that one who flouted the norm of behaviour so tastelessly had placed himself beyond serious discussion.

21 Confused presentation

THE preceding chapters have been concerned with sources of outright misunderstanding, the situation where the receiver ascribes a meaning to a message at variance with that intended by the sender. For every occasion of this sort there are probably a dozen where the impact of a message is blurred or blunted, where the receiver either extracts a confused notion of what he is expected to understand or takes an unnecessarily long time to reach the core of the message. While the barriers already mentioned may contribute to these states, there are other sources whose effects are to reduce the efficiency of communication rather than to distort it completely.

We may consider first the losses that occur from different ways of presenting the same message. Several investigators (Burt (19), Patterson, Poulton (89), Tinker) have made psychological studies of typography, examining the effects of such variables as length of line, or style and size of type, in terms of speed of assimilation and effective retention. While it is not possible to generalize from these studies without regard to the nature of the reading population or of the material presented, statistically significant differences have been found within the contexts of the individual experiments. In particular it has been noted that while the manifestation of a single variable (size of type or length of line) may make no difference, their simultaneous manipulation sometimes does so; in other words, there is interaction between the variables. Poulton's experiments were concerned with the reading of technical material by scientists. A passage was set up in four different print conditions, all frequently used in scientific journals, i.e. none if presented by itself would be likely to excite adverse comment. None the less, one of the four conditions stood out as unquestionably superior from the point of comprehension.

From a single unvaried message we may turn to modifications within the limits of a text whose main elements remain unchanged. Conrad (28) has examined this situation in terms of a standard Post Office instruction card explaining how to use a private telephone network. The item selected for special study concerned the manœuvre of transferring a call from outside the building to another person inside it without going through the operator. Four groups of subjects of approximately equal intelligence received the instruction in the following ways: Group A received the original printed card; Group B the same instruction, but typed more clearly and with wider spacing; Group C were presented with the three sentences which specifically referred to this one manœuvre (in the original the third sentence was separated from the first two by nine lines of print which dealt with something else); Group D were given a full typed version of the original, but with the three critical sentences brought together under a single heading. The twenty members of each group were asked to carry out the manœuvre in question on the basis of their respective instructions. The numbers executing the instructions correctly were:

Group A	Printed original	4
Group B	Typed original	7
Group C	Shortened version	15
Group D	Reworded version	14

The differences due to style of reproduction (A and B) and to amount of information presented (C and D) were not statistically significant, but that between B and D, whose instructions were identical apart from the position of the third critical sentence, was found to be so.

The elements of syntax structure offer another field of exploration. Wason (105, 106, 107) has conducted a series of experiments on the processing of positive and negative information. In the first he set out to establish the response times to four kinds of statement resulting from the combination of two dichotomous variables (true-false, positive-negative). The mean times were:

True affirmatives	8·99 seconds
False affirmatives	11·09 seconds
True negatives	12·58 seconds
False negatives	15·17 seconds

These results were confirmed in a second set of experiments from which an element termed lack of specificity had been removed. In the first study only one pattern of stimuli could have made an affirmative true and a negative false, whereas more than one pattern could have made an affirmative false and a negative true.

Further studies, in collaboration with Jones, examined two possible reasons for the difference in response latencies to affirmative and negative statements: a tendency to translate negative statements into affirmative form and so introduce additional stages in information processing; and a tendency to inhibit response to negative statements because of prohibitive connotations associated with the word 'not'. Whatever the mechanisms involved, it seems beyond doubt that negative statements elicit a longer response time than positive ones, at least where the subject is required to assent or dissent from the statements' truth. Where the subject is required to assimilate information without making any judgement about its truth, the position is not so clear. Compare, for example, '5 doesn't follow 13'—simple assimilation— with 'If 5 doesn't follow 13, put a tick in the box'—assimilation plus assent or dissent.

The practical implications of Wason's and Jones' studies for the design of documents intended for general consumption have been pointed out by Jones in a *New Society* article with the title 'Why can't leaflets be logical?' (58). In the same article she draws attention to the difficulty in understanding passages in which connective words like if, or, but, despite, otherwise, except and unless are too freely employed. The reader gets lost because he has to remember an increasing number of qualifications, many of which are irrelevant to his own case. The following excerpt from the first page of a leaflet on maternity benefits brings these points home:

> 'A marriage which is polygamous cannot be recognized for National Insurance purposes and consequently in such a case a claim cannot be based on the husband's insurance. However, a claim for maternity grant on the husband's insurance may be accepted despite the fact that the marriage took place under a law which allows polygamy in a case where a marriage which took place outside the United Kingdom has, in fact, been monogamous throughout.'

(Leaflet N.I.17A, 'Maternity benefits', 1958)

H

The article suggests that continuous prose is an unsuitable vehicle for communications of this type. Instead, the possibilities of the logical tree, a sequence of simple statements beginning with the most general and ending with the most particular, should be examined. 'In principle, any consistent set of rules can be put in this form, expressed either as a "visual graph", resembling a family tree, or a series of linked statements.'

The last example suggests two themes of relevance to clear presentation. First, difficulty of comprehension can be caused by the over-use of grammatical constructions that are perfectly straightforward when employed in moderation. There is nothing specially difficult about the idea of a negation or a condition, nor is the passage quoted grammatically incorrect. But when conditions and negations are stretched end to end, the strain of assimilation soon becomes excessive. This leads to the second theme, choice of an appropriate medium. If connected prose is used in such a way that the reader is required to assume unduly contorted mental postures, a more fitting medium should be sought. Until fairly recently education and instruction of all kinds have been dominated by verbal text and speech. This state became challenged some forty years ago by a movement in favour of the visual aid, to which diagrams, pictures, films, television have all contributed. The movement is justified because the alternation of media revivifies the attention, while some themes lend themselves more readily to visual presentation than verbal description.

Visual presentation can, of course, be overdone; the inexpert user of charts and diagrams often fails to resist the temptation to try and say too much at a time. The keynote of nearly all successful diagrammatic presentation lies in simplicity of design and absence of cluttering detail. A sequence of logically developed charts is invariably preferable to a single monsterpiece, which in saying everything conveys nothing.

The issue is further complicated by the fact that individuals are differently attuned to different media. There are visualizers, verbalizers and spatializers, each with their biased modes of assimilation. Hence there can be no ideal way of imparting complex information to all comers. The purveyor of information should bear these differences in mind, trying as far as possible to leave no kind of receiver out of account.

The principles of clear presentation are of great importance to education. Among the bad teacher's faults may be mentioned faulty emphasis, the wrong ordering of material, the inclusion of material that is inessential, a poor choice of words and an unfortunate delivery. In saying this, we do not imply that the qualities of good teaching can all be reduced to a capacity for transmitting information. Great teachers have at times been guilty of these failings and have in spite of them fired their students with enthusiasm; but such achievements can hardly be prescribed for.

It is not only the mediocre and inadequate who lack the skill to communicate. From time to time we hear of men of the highest distinction who have been similarly afflicted. It is hard to account for such paradoxes, and the temptation to invoke psychiatric commonplaces in explanation should be resisted. Niels Bohr and Montagu Norman (to mention two eminent non-communicators) may or may not have experienced exceptional psychic tensions. For all we know, such tensions (if they existed) may have constituted a condition of their achievement, and their removal might have turned their possessors into able but commonplace people. At less exalted levels much can be done to raise the quality of instruction by eliminating the faults noted, just as the value of textbooks can be enhanced by improving the logic of their structure.

22 Absence of communication channels

MANY failures in daily communication spring from the absence of any means to bring potential senders and receivers into contact. This barrier is of a different order from those we have so far discussed and only concerns the psychologist in a tangential sort of way. He may, for example, be in a position to point out that facilities for communication are more apparent than real, or that the effect merely of setting up new facilities may be to overload some elements in the organization.

What is in effect a one-way communication system can at times masquerade as something more reciprocal, e.g. the lecturer's 'Any questions?', the commanding officer's 'Any complaints?' Even if the questioner is genuinely anxious to hear the other point of view, his position and prestige may make spontaneous response impossible. It might appear that non-respondents are victims of such a situation, since it is they whose ideas and feelings remain unexpressed. But where authority is intelligent the loss on its side will be as great, since it is left in ignorance and is unable to decide what action is needed to heal a situation it is concerned to set right.

Committees and delegations designed to represent the interests of large groups sometimes end by losing contact with those they are supposed to serve. This happens frequently in industrial disputes, where the machinery of negotiation can become so complex that workers act in defiance of their unions. When the background to such actions is examined, it is often found that some failure to transmit or explain lies at the root of the trouble.

The provision of facilities in a complex organization sometimes calls for amendments to the existing structure. It is not merely that A (whether ministry, division or individual) has not been receiving information which the performance of its duties clearly need; it may be rather that no one's duties have been defined so as to take account of information that clearly demands attention from somebody.

In a society where the need for information of all sorts is taken for granted, there is a danger that facilities may be set up too readily, and, even more, that facilities that have served their turn will continue to exact time and effort. This applies especially to the retention of forms which call for routine completion.

The last chapter considered the need for designing leaflets in a way the public can readily understand. The same arguments apply with equal force to the preparation of many forms and returns. The difficulty of designing a form in such a way that those who complete it supply information meaningful to the recipient is much greater than is generally appreciated.

As organizations grow more complex and the handling of affairs affecting the individual more impersonal, it is to be expected that the individual will at times develop anxiety about the fate of the information that concerns him, or may even begin to wonder if his case has become confused with another's. This rational fear should be borne in mind by those who communicate directly with members of the public. The importance of this is coming to be recognized in the Civil Service, whose style of correspondence has undergone great change in recent years; it is relevant also to many of the professions, to say nothing of commercial and business houses.

23 Instances of failure described and discussed

THIS chapter considers a selection of situations, each of which entails some measure of communication failure. The descriptions are brief and non-technical; some of them can bear more than one interpretation and none could be diagnosed fully without further information. The situations are drawn from a wide human context, and the reader may care to make his own analysis of the probable sources of failure before he looks at the short discussions on the ensuing pages.

Case 1

A clerk finds persistent difficulty in achieving the standards of speed and accuracy set by his colleagues.

Case 2

Two able bridge-players who have not previously played together reach an inappropriate contract of seven diamonds.

Case 3

A teacher, with a reputation for thorough knowledge of his subject, is unable to impart it to his pupils.

Case 4

A father and son are at odds. Each says that the other refuses to consider his point of view.

Case 5

Two art students come to blows over the merits of contemporary and traditional art.

Case 6

A behaviourist and a gestaltist cannot agree about the nature of perception.

Case 7

A writer is obsessed with ideas he finds great difficulty in communicating.

Case 8

A radar operator observes a large number of signals on his screen. He takes no action thinking, 'No one told me there was to be an exercise'. A few minutes later an intense aerial bombardment begins.

Case 9

The managers of a firm are concerned about its inefficiency and low morale and feel that an investigation is called for.

Case 10

A political leader whose candour and integrity are recognized by all, and whose intelligence and command of words are not in question, fails to make an impact on television.

Case 1—The clerk

The simplest explanation is a low general ability which prevents the clerk from processing information at an acceptable speed; in other words, the barrier lies in the limitation of the receiver's capacity. In diagnosing an actual instance it would, however, be important not to leap straight to this or any other conclusion.

We have not been told if the clerk is 20 or 70, male or female, healthy or sickly, outgoing or sullen. The same result could be produced or at least accentuated by some physical handicap (e.g. bad sight), or a personality problem such as general emotional disturbance, exaggerated perfectionism, or acute lack of confidence.

In a task where each man works on his own, standards of acceptability do not constitute an absolute, as they may do with an operator who forms an integral part of a finely adjusted communication system. In the latter case, a slow or inaccurate worker may disrupt the efficiency of the whole system; in the former, he may be better than none and yet be unpopular with colleagues whose load is increased through his shortcomings. In practice there is usually a considerable range in the efficiency and productiveness among those found adequate or better than adequate.

Case 2—The bridge-players

All games depend upon the acceptance of rules by the players. These rules may vary at different times and places, but for a given game each player must be aware of the set holding for that occasion. The observation of rules is the responsibility of an umpire, who should draw the attention of players to any possible source of confusion before the game starts.

In bridge, in addition to rules, there are bidding conventions which each pair is free to choose, provided that the partners make their choice known before a rubber begins. In practice, players sometimes forget to be fully explicit and a situation may arise for which they have failed to make provision and for which no natural bid can be found. A conventional bid may, however, be ambiguous; that is to say, it may refer to more than one system. Thus 'four no trumps' rarely means that the bidder wants to play in four no trumps, which would be a natural bid; usually it is intended to convey slam possibilities. In addition it conveys information about the high cards, and this information varies from one system to another. If the convention has not been agreed before play, it cannot be discussed later and the partner is left to guess. Thus the bidder who uses an ambiguous bid is guilty of an unstated assumption.

Case 3—The teacher

Two distinct lines of explanation come to mind here. First, everything to do with the lecturing situation may disturb this teacher's equilibrium. He dreads the limelight of the platform, fears to excite ridicule, is inaudible and incoherent, imputes hostility to his audience, and shrinks from displaying his merchandise before it. These factors make him unable to communicate not merely with his hearers but even with himself; in such an environment he cannot organize or express what he has to say. This is a failure of expression resulting from a combination of social influences to which the personality is unable to adjust; the same man in the quiet of his study would have no difficulty in setting out his material. A failure of this type cannot be traced to any of the defects we have been discussing, though it may embody nearly all of them. The root of the trouble lies in social adaptation, not in the mechanics of communication.

The second explanation might be that the teacher's presentation, though lucid and polished, fails to get across to his pupils to whom he has ascribed a background of knowledge which they lack. To an audience in possession of the necessary information his lecture might be masterly; to one without it, his sentences arouse at best an impotent admiration. It may be that he projects his own state of knowledge to his hearers and that he is in effect talking to himself rather than them. Or he may engender an emotional atmosphere which is dissipated the moment he finishes. A listener might then say, 'I thought I understood while he was talking, but I can't remember anything he said.' This is an instance of the unstated assumption on a grand scale.

Case 4—Father and son

There are factors that may at any time strain relations between the members of different generations. The older man may resent the younger's vigour, his speed of repartee, his stores of recently acquired knowledge; the younger is sometimes jealous of the other's poise, authority and possessions. These are not direct causes of communication failure, but they supply a soil where it can readily develop. The direct cause is likely to be schema incompatibility, perhaps at the intellectual level as a result of different educational systems, almost certainly at the level of attitude and valuation. The older man's outlook may be based on values that commanded acceptance thirty years earlier; to his son they appear pompous fictions unvalidated by the facts of living.

Case 5—The art students

The controversies that have raged over 'modern' art since 1900 were based originally on two misunderstandings, namely that the artist's job was to represent nature and that he aimed to create 'beauty'. Both these aims have been strenuously repudiated by numerous painters and sculptors, but their denials have not brought the enlightenment the exposure of an unstated assumption usually does. How is this to be accounted for? As long as the representational tradition lasted, natural objects supplied what many took to be a criterion of good and bad art. The removal of this reference point was like depriving a blind man of his stick. Without external reality to refer to, the non-artist found himself disoriented. Unless he had special insight or training, he could not fall back on the internal properties of design and balance which to the artist supply a criterion independent of subject matter.

When the non-artist talks of painting 'beauty', he means representing objects in a way that excites pleasing and peaceful sensations. This notion holds no meaning for an artist concerned to express his reactions to the life around him. He is far more anxious to stimulate than to soothe, and he strongly resists the idea that his function is to please. Art may have served this purpose in times of peaceful contentment, but in periods of turbulent transition the artist may well feel it his task to make the less sensitive and perceptive aware of their predicament rather than to dope them with palliatives. If he thinks in terms of social purpose, he will conceive his own as giving expression to latent stirrings in the general consciousness. In doing this, his realization of the forces in his environment will frequently be interpreted as disintegration within his own personality; this will often amount to a misreading of the situation, since there is little evidence of association between hyper-sensitivity and neuroticism. Some artists, on the other hand, may work to express a private vision, caring little for the reactions of others; they do not think of their work as communication, except perhaps to themselves and a few who chance to be similarly attuned.

Case 6—Behaviourist and gestaltist

If perception is the basic feature of mental life, it is probable that every psychologist must hold some theory about its nature, even though the theory may not be made explicit. Conversely, if a psychologist's views about perception are known, it is often possible to infer his orientation towards other problems. Perception, whether conceived statically as a unit or dynamically as a process, is the main link between the subject and his environment; it is, if we may speak metaphorically, the medium through which the external world communicates with the conscious organism.

Science is often presented as a system for the establishment of solid and reliable knowledge; this, no doubt, is its long-term objective, but in practice the individual working scientist requires to adopt a model, a view of how phenomena are related, before he can exert a grip on the external or internal world. There is no one model, no single way of viewing reality, so that the model an individual adopts is to some extent the result of choice, the factors that decide this choice including subjective as well as objective considerations. A model, or at least a paradigm, is a necessity for all exploratory thinking and, once adopted, it is likely to exert a strengthening hold on the thinker. To discard a paradigm that has done years of service and to invent a new one free of the old influence demands a power of adjustment few possess. The situation is in some ways comparable to that of an artist who renounces the style that has brought him fame to build a new reputation in what is virtually a different medium.

Behaviourism and gestalt were both reactions from the atomistic introspective outlook which dominated the psychological scene in the first years of the century. Gestalt repudiated atomism in favour of a holistic approach which held that the act of perception was unmediated by learning; behaviourism repudiated introspection, arguing that the only study worth pursuing was that of objectively observed behaviour. Terms like insight and spontaneous awareness held no meaning for the behaviourist, who saw them as the hallucinations of a neo-introspectionist mythology.

Thus the behaviourist's set predisposes him to see evidence of learning, whereas the gestaltist is predisposed to the notion of unmediated experience. How deep do these predispositions go? Are they the product of attitudes acquired early in life or the cause of the adoption of attitudes that harmonize with early assumptions? Whatever the answer, similar oppositions have dominated intellectual life throughout the centuries, e.g. Fluxionism (Heracleitus) v. Permanentism (Parmenides), Nominalism v. Realism, Scepticism (Hume) v. A Priorism (Kant), Logical Positivism (Carnap) v. Philosophy of Organism (Whitehead). All these oppositions have led men of the highest ability to present irreconcilable accounts of the same phenomena and to achieve almost total failure in their efforts to communicate with one another. Where holders of opposing views are genuinely unable to come to terms, it seems that the root cause must be traced to what has been called incompatibility of schemas.

Case 7—The writer

Every apprentice writer has difficulty in fitting words to thoughts; this is the problem of the craftsman learning his trade. But some who by everyday standards have learned their trade, who have established their professional role, continue to experience difficulty whenever they put pen to paper. This is the situation of many literary artists under pressure to express new ideas and unable to live on old experience. Whereas competence operates from a baseline of well-entrenched schemas, originality entails the regrouping of old ones and the fashioning of new ones; it does not merely solve presented problems, it formulates fresh strata of understanding and feeling.

This is one aspect of the story; the other concerns the traffic between different levels of experience. Originality is dependent on free traffic between the regions of fantasy and rationality. The conditions that make this possible are rarely met; it is as though there existed a natural enmity between these extremes of experience. The layman who backs his hunch in the face of reason and evidence and the intellectual who rejects evidence that conflicts with theory are opponents in the same game. For art or science to be creative, the images of fantasy and the ideas of reason must be free to shuttle to and fro like barges on a river.

Case 8—The radar operator

The operator sees the signals and knows that they mean the approach of aircraft. His previous experience of such displays has been limited to exercises by his own air force simulating an enemy attack. He has always been told when these exercises are to take place and his instructions are that such notice will always be given. In spite of the absence of any notice he decides, with catastrophic results, that no action is called for. On the information given, we cannot be sure how far his failure is cognitive (interpreting present in terms of past experience) or affective (refusal to accept the implications of a correct interpretation).

Case 9—Firm with poor morale

The investigation may reveal that part, or even all, of the trouble has originated in failure to analyse the total situation, allocate precise responsibilities to individuals and lay down channels for the conveyance of information. Only in the very smallest groups —and not always in those—can information flow automatically to the people who should receive it. Organization becomes necessary at the point where incoming messages are too many for a single man to handle. To plan a division of labour which ensures that information reaches the right people without burdening those it does not concern is one of a management's main tasks. Among the chief faults arising from defective communication are the taking of incompatible decisions by different people, the failure to take decisions or to take them at the right time, the frustration of those whose efforts get ignored, distorted or misunderstood, the overloading of individuals with irrelevant information, and the demoralization of those whose ability is underemployed.

Case 10—The political leader

Words like photogenic and telegenic originated in the discrepancies found between ordinary visual impressions and the images projected by some people on plate or screen. Such discrepancies excite comment because of the assumption that it is the purpose of camera, film and television to provide substitutes for visual perception. The discovery that these media create images of their own has never been readily accepted; if they improve on or detract from the representation of someone we know, it is the familiar representation that supplies our criterion and the new media that are held to distort.

The position is different with public figures, who are rarely seen directly and whose images are built up through secondary media. Here the photogenic, whatever their real-life appearance, gain an enormous advantage, while their less fortunate rivals forgo their normal natural qualities.

The likely reasons for communication failure in these ten cases may be summarized as follows:

Case	Probable reason for failure
1 Clerk	Limitation of receiver's capacity
2 Bridge-players	Unstated assumption (single)
3 Teacher	a) Lack of social adaptation
	b) Unstated assumption (multiple)
4 Father and son	Schema incompatibility
5 Art students	Unstated assumptions derived from schema incompatibility
6 Behaviourist and gestaltist	Schema incompatibility
7 Writer	Original expression calls for reorganization of schemas
8 Radar operator	Wrong interpretation of message probably due to unconscious resistance
9 Firm with poor morale	Lack of communication facilities
10 Political leader	Distortion of image by new medium

PART THREE

Communication Problems in Complex Activities

24 Personnel selection

THIS section is designed to give some idea of the range of communication issues in real-life situations. The choice of activities is arbitrary and the discussions do not pretend to be exhaustive. One or two facets of each activity are highlighted, the rest ignored, the intention being to provide a panoramic view of the information field.

The transmission of information plays a major role in all complex activities, from the acquisition and exercise of individual skill to the administration of international affairs. In the former, particularly where the skill entails a large psychomotor element (as in nearly all forms of sport), much of the information is generated internally, skill being readily acquired by those with quick and well-integrated proprioceptive cues.

Our main concern, however, is with highly organized activities in which information passes from person to person as a preliminary to the making of decisions. How far decisions flow automatically from the presentation of relevant information and how far they depend upon other factors is a question on which thought is still somewhat confused. It seems likely that those who avoid taking decisions are often shrinking from the labour of assembling the data required to do so, and that when their resistance to this has been overcome the decisions can be made easily. But it would be rash to assume that all decision-making can be reduced to such simple terms.

Personnel selection is one of many situations where professional advice is sought, and much that is said about it will apply to other types of applied research. Its goal, like that of most scientific enterprise, is prediction, but the predictions concern the behaviour of individuals rather than of classes of people or equipment.

This is by no means the first attempt to study selection as a communication problem. As long ago as 1951 Hick (50) published a paper called 'Information theory and intelligence tests', while earlier in that year Sir Cyril Burt (17) had included a highly suggestive section on 'The mechanical theory of communication' in a long article entitled 'Test construction and the scaling of items'. Among many illuminating comments he argued that 'the aim of the test constructor is to maximize the amount of information finally secured while minimizing the cost of securing it'.

Selection techniques are concerned to elicit and organize information about persons in relation to various job requirements and to raise continually the proportion of relevant to irrelevant information (called in another context the signal/noise ratio). A candidate may be thought of as the source of a variety of signals deriving from his looks, dress, voice, gestures, etc. It falls to the selector to reduce these to some ordered meaning and to elicit further signals in the form of intellectual or social behaviour. Thus a good test can be thought of as a kind of funnel through which a concentrated stream of relevant information is directed, and a well streamlined interview as a means of obtaining meaningful specimens of social behaviour.

The aim of all selection is to predict the candidate's behaviour in some future context: whether he will succeed or fail, and, if successful, by how much he will perform beyond the minimum requirement. If we apply the information-theory paradigm to this situation, we see that it is the candidate who assumes the role of input provider, the assessor or assessing instrument who corresponds to the communication channel, and the score or assessment that constitutes the output. If at first it seems natural to think of the testing situation as the stimulus and the candidate's performance as output, we should remind ourselves that it is the candidate who supplies the information. The input is supplied by the person or object being tested; the selection instrument only occupies this role during the development and standardization phases. Any tendency to confuse these roles may perhaps be traced to incompatibility between the stimulus-response model, in terms of which the bulk of classical experiments have been conceived, and the systems model, which supplies the pattern for communication theory.

Let us see how the IT paradigm fits old-type and new-type testing. In the first, the questions are framed so widely that they exert little control over the input. An essay question can not merely lead to answers of varying quality; it can also prompt replies along many different lines, some of which will appeal more strongly to one examiner than to another. Hence a given input (answer) can occasion a variety of outputs (scores). Part at least of the reason for this is that no examiner (channel) can hold and compare objectively all possible answers to such a question. To solve this dilemma he is almost bound to select some aspect of the input for special consideration, whether it be factual information, evidence of reasoning ability, style, imagination or even handwriting. Such dissipation of interest is automatically avoided in a new-type test, which is designed so that each input (selection from a finite number of stated answers) gives rise to a consistent output (correct or incorrect answer).

It will be clear that where a human being acts as a communication channel, the factors that may contaminate input are far more complex than those in a mechanical or electronic system. In the latter, input may be masked or lost through the intrusion of unwanted impulses, but distortion through the selective operation of noise is not a normal risk. With a human channel, the distortion of input can come about in many ways. Overloading can itself be a cause, as when an unskilled interviewer, overwhelmed by a candidate's verbosity, clutches at some irrelevant straw to help him sustain his position. A less crude way of dealing with excessive load occurs when the dominance of one sense modality leads to the discarding of data from another. Distortion can, of course, occur when there is no question of overload. When an interviewer is unduly impressed by a single aspect of behaviour—verbal fluency, say, or the candidate's interest in sailing—it need not be because he is intellectually incapable of absorbing fresh evidence, but because some biasing factor has taken charge of the situation. When this happens there is not merely loss of output; the output that emerges (a biased judgement) will be a construct fashioned from an arbitrarily chosen fragment of input. These types of distortion are more likely to come about when the human being is operating with many degrees of freedom (as when he is evaluating the performance of a candidate) than when he is acting as a link in a closed system (relaying calls on a switchboard), though even here it would be rash to assume that errors are wholly unrelated to personality factors.

Our argument suggests that the successes of scientific selection are closely related to the control of input in testing and inter-viewing situations. In testing we ensure through our choice of questions that the information supplied by the subject relates to homogeneous material and that the presentation of his answers is restricted to a choice among the prescribed alternatives. A trained interviewer has learned to distinguish relevant and irrelevant information; he has been taught how to elicit what is relevant and has been supplied with a clear-cut goal of inquiry. The effect of all this is to make far better use of his capacities for holding information; because the input he has to deal with is now largely controlled, there is more likelihood of the output being reliable.

Control of input is not, of course, an end in itself. If it were, any objective test could be used as a predictor for any type of task. The mistake of grasping at a yardstick because it is a yardstick is a temptation to be strongly resisted, since it is axiomatic that the choice of selection instruments rests upon job analysis in the beginning and subsequently upon validation study.

There are still many unsolved problems in selection. One possi-bility of advance lies in the suggestion that the multiple-choice test works within too confined limits to tap some of the more elusive abilities. If this proves to be the case, psychologists will be faced with the difficulty of making a more open type of test psychometrically respectable. Some will argue that the success that has been achieved with multiple-choice type tests (sometimes referred to as convergent) is directly related to the substitution of a closed for an open item structure; if this is so, the problem just stated seems to involve an inherent contradiction. Against this the protagonists of the open-ended (divergent) test claim to have established acceptable reliabilities for their measures and significant differences between the performances of contrasted groups of subjects (e.g. arts and science students). This claim is interpreted as meaning that success in arts subjects is more dependent on fertility of ideas and associations than on controlled thinking.

Other sources of weakness lie in the meagre contribution so far made by personality as opposed to ability measures. There are also unsolved problems in the criterion area. The value of a selection instrument can only be established against some external standard; if these standards are themselves unstable, the demonstrable value of selection is correspondingly limited.

So far selection has been discussed solely from the standpoint of the selector. There are also aspects of communication that concern the candidate. Though these are of a less technical nature, they should not be overlooked on that account. Whatever the predictive power of testing procedures, there is an impersonality about them which the face-to-face interview can do much to redress. In other words, the retention of the interview in selection should not be judged solely on its assessment value. The interviewer is regarded as a representative of the organization he serves and the appeal of the organization is largely dependent on the impression he makes. In particular, it is his responsibility to make clear to the candidate the conditions on which he may be employed and his prospects within the organization, so far as they can be estimated.

25 Literary criticism

A RECENT number of *The Author*, the organ of the Society of Authors, contains nearly a dozen letters on the subject of reviewing, and particularly of the alleged inadequacies of reviews that do not carry the names or initials of the reviewers. Whether these shortcomings are the result of anonymity or whether they are apt to appear equally in signed notices is an open question; the fact that stands out is that many authors believe themselves to be the victims of critics who have made little or no attempt to come to grips with the work they are discussing. One author asserts that roughly a third of the reviews of his latest book could have been written entirely from the publisher's blurb, 'two of them doing no more than reproduce the blurb virtually word for word'.

We must not fall into the trap of assuming that the sole purpose of a critical column is to record objective comparisons; part of the critic's function is to stimulate and entertain, and the bare pronouncement of a considered judgement, however valid, is not in itself exciting. Further, the conditions under which many reviewers work are known to be arduous (a play or film nearly every night, half a dozen books in a weekly column), and it would be absurd to ignore such factors. All that is suggested is that someone who examines the processes of communication and judgement formation may be able to throw an occasional beam on the problems of critical expertise.

There is sufficient common ground between the goals of the critics and the personnel selector to justify a brief analysis of the main points of likeness and divergence. The basic similarity lies in the fact that each is required to evaluate individual cases, whether people or books, and that the basis of judgement is information derived from the case to be judged. To do this, each has to thread his way through an informational bombardment where there is a continual need to discriminate relevant from irrelevant, essential from inessential. Sharp differences immediately spring to mind: the selector has to predict behaviour in relation to specific tasks, the critic to give a general judgement of value; the critic assesses what is put before him, the selector has to elicit behaviour; the selector seeks to substitute objective measuring instruments for personal impressions, the critic is seen as an expert with perceptions refined by interest and practice; the selector expresses his findings in near mathematical language, the literary critic presents his in the medium he is criticizing; and, as implied above, the selector is under no obligation to make his judgements sound interesting, while the critic's functions include the requirement to be readable and even provocative.

If a book is regarded as a communication from writer to reader, we can see two broad ways in which the reader can go astray in evaluating it; he may fail to receive the communication in the way the writer intended, or he may receive it correctly and misrate its worth. The second of these problems does not directly concern us, but the first is a clear communication issue that we should attempt to consider. If we take a book we know well and set our own assessment of it against judgements at variance with ours, we find two main sources of divergence: we may consider that the critic's view has been distorted because he has attached undue importance to some parts of the book at the expense of other parts, or we may decide that, without being guilty of specific distortion, he has assumed the purpose of the writer to be something different from what we take it to be. We are not, of course, asserting that our own view is the right one; the error may well be ours.

Each of the above deviations can occur in a number of ways and at several levels of understanding. Instances of the part-for-whole fallacy would include the musical critic who assesses a performance of *Rhinegold* by the steadiness of the horn passages in the first twenty bars, the pedant who counts typographical errors in an imaginative novel, the dramatic critic who arrives at the end of Act I and spends Act III in the bar.

A sophisticated variant occurs when two reviewers select the same aspects of a work for mention but evaluate them in opposing ways. The following notices of a novel about India include no less than three such oppositions:

1) 'Mr T.'s writing is direct and unaffected. I could not believe in his lovers for a moment, but his descriptive powers are of a high order.' *Guardian*

2) 'Mr T. tells in level, undistinguished prose of a pilgrimage made to Banaras by a young Hindu doctor, who knows he is dying, and an English girl he meets on the road. She falls in love with him and Mr T. succeeds in making her devotion moving and credible, yet too often the novel reads like either a guidebook or an elementary introduction to Hindu beliefs.' *The Times*

In these two notices almost diametrically opposing valuations are found in regard to (*a*) the general quality of the writing, (*b*) the credibility of the love affair, and (*c*) the writer's descriptive skill.

The ascription of wrong intention can also come about in many ways. Queen Victoria, baffled by her inability to laugh at Lewis Carroll's mathematical treatises, is a far cry from the *literati* who complained that Sir Thomas Wyatt (46) had no ear for metre. The sole point of contact is that both assessors were making a false assumption; Carroll wasn't trying to write a sequel to *Through the Looking Glass* and Wyatt wasn't trying to write regular octosyllabics.

It will be appreciated that these two categories are meant to be no more than broadly descriptive; assignment of a specific instance to either category tells nothing of the psychological mechanisms that have prompted it. Many could be explained in terms of the barriers of Part 2, though even these lay no claim to psychological finality. Of course, the receipt of a communication of a hundred thousand words is likely to introduce complications unusual in that of a simple statement.

While there is no question of trying to turn criticism into a science, there can be no harm in asking if statistical techniques can make any contribution to the critic's task. Most of the studies so far carried out on language and verbal behaviour have been concerned with factual rather than valuational judgements; e.g. Yule's book *The Statistical Study of Literary Vocabulary* (119) counts and compares the length of sentences in two works with a view to determining identity of authorship. This issue is of obvious importance to the world of literary scholarship but irrelevant to the quality of the works in question. Miller's chapter on individual differences in his *Language and Communication* (76) comes nearer to the matter of personal style, as when he quotes Thorndike's table showing the relative frequencies per 1,000 punctuation marks for fourteen authors:*

	,	.	;	:	—	( )	...	?	!
18th century									
Defoe	718	134	121	10	4	3	0	8	2
Richardson	534	161	85	37	65	34	0	33	51
Fielding	584	198	119	14	22	19	0	28	13
Jane Austen	522	270	92	6	31	4	0	2	4
19th century									
Scott	687	177	58	1	48	1	0	12	12
Thackeray	569	213	64	22	44	20	0	30	3
Dickens	583	233	57	12	35	20	0	25	34
Meredith	466	336	58	25	29	4	6	32	44
Hardy	510	323	55	9	41	6	3	31	20
20th century									
Edith Wharton	433	302	65	31	70	7	15	50	27
Wells	441	337	30	3	53	1	32	30	31
Bennett	440	368	31	20	19	8	7	37	69
Galsworthy	447	292	61	28	58	5	1	38	70
Angela Thirkell	586	368	4	5	3	2	0	28	9

Miller comments: 'Clear stylistic differences are apparent. Some of these differences depend upon what sort of persons and events the author writes about and what sort of readers he writes for. Some differences are merely the operations of fashions in punctuation. But even when allowances are made for these factors, large stylistic differences remain. In artistic writing, punctuation does more than guide the reader's pauses and aid his recognition of grammatical structure; punctuation influences emphasis, movement, style.' This is reasonable enough, but the critic still has a long way to go before he can make a meaningful interpretation of the habits of period or author; it may be significant that '...' makes its appearance around 1860 and that Angela Thirkell virtually bans the semi-colon, but how do we go on to establish what such things mean?

A somewhat more positive contribution may perhaps be found

* Reprinted from G. A. Miller's *Language and Communication* (1963) by permission of McGraw-Hill Publishing Company Ltd.

in an approach described in a paper read to the British Psychological Society by the present writer in 1947 (85). Arguing that criticism is concerned above everything with the differentiating characteristics of the writer and his work, he set out to determine the incidence of the commonest nouns as used by a representative sample of English poets, the list to act as a control against which the incidences of individual poets could be compared. When 100 lines (ten sections of ten lines)were taken from the works of twenty poets, the following table resulted:

Nouns with incidence of 10 or more per 1,000 lines

Man	31	God ⎫		Life	11
Love	19	Heart ⎬ 13			
Eye	18			Death ⎫	
Day ⎫		Thing	12	Hand ⎬ 10	
Soul ⎬ 14·5				Light ⎭	
Time ⎭		Heaven	11·5		

A count was then made for two contemporary poets (not, incidentally, included in the control sample), taking a thousand lines from each. The resultant lists are shown on the opposite page.

Inspection suggests one or two moderately interesting things. Words like man, eye and day figure with about the same frequency in all three lists. Time appears four times as often in the Eliot list as in the control or Davies; death, end, church, fire, wind, bone and way are prominent with Eliot, but do not figure in the others. Love does not appear in Eliot's list, God does not figure in Davies'. The following words appear in Davies' list alone: joy, bird, face, tree, night, body, music, stone, child, mind, friend, thought, woman, sun, year.

Some may question our initial comparison between personnel selection and criticism on the ground that the first has established itself as a branch of applied science while the second has not, is not likely to, probably should not try to. But there are few activities that cannot be in some way enlightened by the application of scientific principles, even if there is no question of their becoming branches of applied science. It is important that they should be brought under such an examination, however limited the scope for experiment may be. Analysis in the light of well-established principles can alone do something to assist practice.

Nouns with incidence of 10 or more per 1,000 lines
Poetry of T. S. Eliot

Time	58	Place ⎫	12	Bone ⎫	
Man	29	Voice ⎭		Day	
Eye	19			Light ⎬ 10	
Death	18	Church ⎫		Way ⎭	
End	17	Fire ⎬	11		
God ⎫	14	Wind ⎭			
World ⎭					

Poetry of W. H. Davies

Man	46	Night ⎫	14	Friend ⎫	
Love	25	Time ⎭		Thought ⎬ 11	
Day	21			Voice	
Life	20	Body ⎫		Woman ⎭	
Joy	18	Music ⎬	13		
Eye	17	Stone		Light ⎫	
Bird ⎫		World ⎭		Place ⎬ 10	
Face ⎬ 16				Sun	
Tree ⎭		Child ⎫		Year ⎭	
Heaven 15		Death ⎬	12		
		Mind ⎭			

26 Education and training

TRADITIONAL educational methods have sustained heavy criticism over the past decades. On the one hand it has been argued that communication from teacher to pupil has left much to be desired, on the other that education has been conceived too exclusively as a communication issue. These two lines of attack are complementary rather than contradictory; both spring from a deeper and more positive concept of education than obtained fifty years ago.

The arguments on the communication aspect include two already cited, that information has been purveyed in too exclusively verbal a manner, and that no adequate provision has been made for the pupil to confront the teacher with his difficulties. Perhaps the basic criticism is that the pupil has been regarded as a passive recipient, the able scholar being the child who absorbs most and asks least. Woven into this attitude has been the insidious notion that learning is an inherently distasteful and hence morally elevating task. This idea has even led some psychologists to argue that the concept of motivation is an artifact of distraught teachers desperate to find a way of reinforcing their sanctions.

Recent trends have emphasized the need to present learning material to the student in as logical a way as possible, to make use of visual examples when the opportunity offers, to reduce rote learning to a minimum, and to encourage the student to bring his learning difficulties into the open. It has been argued that large classes are an unhappy necessity brought about by economic stringencies and a dearth of suitable teachers. The ideal situation is held to be that of the individual tutor, who can adapt instruction to his pupil's natural tempo; the class of thirty and above with pupils of several levels of ability and attainment is an unhappy compromise, offering little or no incentive to brighter students and leaving duller ones in a state of progressive bewilderment.

The second criticism proceeds from the belief that to think of instruction solely in terms of the conveyance of information is to divorce education from the realities of living. Education, it is argued, is essentially an activity in which the pupil must participate, irrespective of age or ability. A system which divides the material of study into a number of unrelated subjects, presented abstractedly in a series of verbal texts, possesses no lasting value for the development of mind or character. Its sole justification is the acquisition of certificates of examination, which society has been persuaded to accept as evidence of proficiency.

These strictures have been applied to the teaching of every subject, from Latin to geography, arithmetic to French, poetry to grammar. Charges of surreptitious propaganda have been alleged additionally over topics like scripture and English history. Discipline, rote learning and suggestion were, in the view of the severer critics, the chief pillars of education till recent years, and anyone who came through an average school curriculum before 1940 is likely to admit a great measure of truth in the charges. In spite of this, there have always been individuals who have emerged from these ordeals with a thirst for learning and scholarship. How this survival can be accounted for—whether in terms of intelligence, dedication, or the influence of one or two exceptional teachers—is hard to say. If the criticisms seem unduly harsh, it is fair to ask how many Englishmen, after eight or ten years' schooling in French, have been able to make themselves understood when they set foot on the continent of Europe. And against this, how few, after three months at a modern language school like Berlitz, have failed to make their needs known.

Contemporary requirements have created special demands for improved methods in the teaching of mathematics, science and languages. In most of these methods the accent has been on meaningful behaviour, whether this takes the form of direct comparison of the student's efforts at pronunciation with the recordings of a native speaker, of relating the arithmetical processes to life situations or coming to grips with science through the medium of individual experiment. In all these approaches dissatisfaction with past methods has been so wide-felt that the need for controlled comparison between old and new methods has to some extent been sidestepped. A more controversial issue like the introduction of a phonetic alphabet in the first reading years is being tested more rigorously, the earliest results suggesting confirmation of the innovators' claims.

While the emphasis in new educational methods is on the pupil's participation and the early development of imagination, that of vocational training is moving away from theory in the direction of specificity; instead of giving a technician a general grounding which he can later apply to a wide variety of situations, the tendency is to train him directly to use a particular piece of equipment. This shift of accent is partly due to the specialization of many new tasks which makes the application of broad principle a far more nebulous business than it used to be, and partly to manpower stringency which compels organizations to make greater use of those with limited ability. The trend forces instructors to isolate the critical elements in a task, directing attention to what the human operator actually does rather than talking in broad terms about the sort of things he may have to do. This pragmatic revolution in training method is clearly justified by the present situation, dominated as it is by continuous technological development that involves frequent change in the use of manpower. But the growing gap between education and training is bound to excite concern; it is, to say the least, ironical that the first should be making concerted effort to realize all-round creative capacity at the moment when the second is reducing job content more and more to the level of routine process.

27 Communication and military decision

THE military commander has been conceived traditionally as the prototype of firm action and quick decision in contrast to the politician, who has been seen as manipulating words to avoid commitment. Although like all stereotypes this oversimplifies the situation, the fact remains that emergency supplies the *raison d'être* of the armed forces, and the need to take swift and irreversible decision lies at the root of many military attitudes, such as the necessity to obey orders without questioning. However desirable it may be for people of conflicting views to meet and negotiate, there are still situations that demand action rather than discussion.

Information theory and decision theory, though distinct mathematical concepts, are products of the same intellectual climate, and the forces that led to their births are closely related. It is the normal function of newly acquired information to assist the recipient to decide some issue. It is, of course, true that information can be pursued for its own sake and that decisions can be taken without a basis of information, but neither of these possibilities alters the fact that the need to improve communication systems is related to the need to make decisions speedily and effectively. It is also true that both these needs have asserted themselves predominantly in wartime situations.

We may start by distinguishing the operator, whose task is bounded by the system he works in, from the commander, who has to relate the information provided by such systems with information received from other sources. Operators and commanders are the source of important communication problems, but these are of a different order.

The operator, under which term are included a considerable range of plotters, trackers, telephonists, clerks, observers and senders of information, is required to handle information effectively within a system of which he is a part. The main obstacles to success in such roles are defective general intelligence, ineptitude in regard to the medium employed, and physical shortcomings in the area of the distance senses, e.g. colour blindness, shortsightedness, deafness. Defining the critical job requirements for this sort of task follows the same pattern as for any other, but the exigencies of new types of display and equipment are continually postulating familiar problems in unfamiliar forms. The question here is not to find which individuals should be barred admittance to an established occupation, but to decide whether a role postulated by some new system can in fact be discharged by a human being, and, if not, whether an alternative method of human performance can be found. Two limited problems (one auditory, one visual) recently studied on behalf of the American Army show the sort of thing we have in mind.

Stichman and Renaud (96) have studied the effects of various procedures on the transcription of word lists received at different signal-to-noise ratios. The performance data consisted of the percentage of words correctly identified under each procedure at each of the four ratios. The experimental design was a 4 by 20 by 12 factorial (4 S-to-N ratios, 20 transcription methods and 12 human subjects), each subject performing under all eighty combinations of the first two factors. The stimulus material consisted of 1,000 monosyllables divided into twenty fifty-word lists. The words in each list were presented at an intensity of 75 decibels every $4\frac{1}{2}$ seconds at S-to-N ratios of +4db, 0, −4db and −8db. The twenty transcription methods were reached by varying the number of presentations of each word list (once, twice, three times), the number of times the subject was required to write each list, and the degree of use of previous written copy permitted to the subject in preparing for the next transcript. The experiments showed (a) that listening to a word list more than once before writing the transcript did not improve performance at any S-to-N ratio, (b) that the subject's use of previous transcripts as reference aids in retranscription nowhere improved performance, but that (c) when subjects both listened to and wrote the word lists more than once, significant improvements resulted.

The visual study (104) was concerned with the effects of information extraction and assimilation brought about by varying the conditions of presentation. Forty-eight subjects were shown successive pairs of slides. The first slide contained twelve, eighteen or twenty-four flag symbols randomly positioned on a map. The second slide was identical with the first, except that two, four or six symbols had been varied. While viewing the second slide, the subjects had to count and identify the information (extraction process); afterwards, to indicate on a replica of the first slide the alterations they had noticed on the second (assimilation). Three different ways of making the changed data conspicuous (hard-copy, single-cue and double-cue coding) were compared with unaided performance. It appeared (a) that performance in both extraction and assimilation was best on slides where symbols had been removed, and worst where they had been repositioned; (b) that double-cue coding greatly, and single-cue coding substantially, improved both extraction and assimilation, whereas hard-copy (i.e. the simultaneous presentation of a copy of the first slide with the second one) led to virtually no improvement. In general, change of information tended to degrade performance, and, as the extent of change increased, omissions were found to increase more rapidly than positive errors.

It will be clear that the number of variables it is possible to manipulate in these presentation experiments is almost endless, and a flair to select the more relevant ones for study will enormously increase the fertility of the results. But even the best experimental work is likely to confirm the obvious ten times for every unexpected finding; the vast energies that go into research are vindicated by the occasional unlooked-for discovery, and, equally important, by finding that the obvious does not accord with fact.

When we turn to the study of tactical and strategical decisions, we sometimes find attention given primarily to qualities of personality (dash, energy, determination), which are held to characterize successful commanders. However important these qualities may be, the emphasis given to them masks the more prosaic facts of the role information plays in forming decisions. The importance of this role is accentuated today by the development of automated methods of data presentation, whose value depends on their acceptance by those in authority. The speed and complexity of events are such that it is virtually impossible to check the reliability of data. On the other hand, the storage mechanisms that lie behind these presentations make it possible to reconstruct at a later date the bases of decisions taken in a way that has hitherto seldom been possible. It is sometimes asked how the commanders of the future will assimilate the benefits of these aids without surrendering some degree of responsibility for the resulting decisions. In the past this acceptance of responsibility has been regarded as a *sine qua non* of leadership. Is this condition now being challenged? If not, how will it be possible to reconcile it with the implications of technical development?

While it is not yet possible to give a full answer to these questions, an attempt can be made to put them in perspective. We can note, for example, that the captain of a modern aircraft is supplied with all kinds of information he has to take on trust; but he still performs an essential role by integrating the different streams of data, and to some extent by relating them to other information he receives more directly. There is no suggestion that in carrying out these tasks he is filling the role of an automaton; although in one sense he has far less freedom of manœuvre in the use of his aircraft, in another the demands made on him as a human being are greater than ever before. More specifically we may note that after an accident has occurred, it is often possible for analysis of the stored records to determine whether it was the result of error by the pilot or due to some other cause; the fact that what would once have remained conjectural can today be made objectively factual has not, however, led to any unreadiness to assume the pilot role.

The trend of these arguments may be illustrated by an example given in a recent article 'Computers at war' (56) in the *New Scientist*:

'During a recent live exercise the radar showed a "hostile" aircraft approaching its target from the south-west at a speed of Mach 1·4, and a height of 35,000 feet. At his desk the controller fed the basic target information into a computer and asked it whether an interception was possible from airfield X, where a fighter stood at combat readiness. The computer indicated "interception go" and the fighter was scrambled. As the enemy aircraft closed in, the computer was constantly calculating and displaying the interception-to-kill point and giving out the necessary interception commands for the fighter pilot. By this means orders and information flowed continuously from controller to fighter.'

This example gives a vivid indication of the roles of controller, computer and pilot, suggesting that those of the two human participants call for high standards of skill and responsibility. It may be that what holds in the restricted context of a single aircraft may prove valid in much wider fields.

28 The administration of law

THE lawmaker's task is basically one of framing generalizations to include all instances of a class of actions, states or conditions while excluding the rest; the difficulty of doing this so as to make sense in terms of individual circumstances or judgements is almost overwhelmingly great. A generalization links together a variety of instances with a single common feature. Even at the simplest cognitive level this procedure is rarely unambiguous; sooner or later there is dispute as to whether a particular object is red or not-red, and the difficulty of defining a term in such a way that it is used the same way by everyone is much greater than might be supposed. This, as pointed out earlier, leads to a certain amount of faulty communication even at an elementary cognitive level. The difficulty would be far more apparent if the purpose of the generalization was to bring about action, if we were not merely concerned to say 'I don't like these books', but 'Any books I don't like must be suppressed'. A rule or law is a generalization of the latter kind; it does not merely specify a group of objects, it goes on to indicate the action that must be taken in respect of them.

So far the lawgiver has been spoken of as a person, but the individual lawmaker (Solon, Moses) is a character rarely met outside small and somewhat primitive societies. In complex societies lawmaking is mainly the work of legislative bodies reinforced by custom.

Most legal systems evolve between the poles of statutory and case law. A statute is a law framed to anticipate some type of event, but because what is nominally the same event can occur in an endless variety of circumstances, some attempt has to be made to tailor the generalization to make it cover this wide range of happenings. This leads as a rule to an act of great complexity hedged with numerous qualifications; even when this has been produced, the statute will still fail to relate in many ways to the intricacy of life situations, so that for a while no lawyer can be sure how some situations will fare when set against it.

Statutory ambiguity opens the door to case law or law by precedent, i.e. to the interpretations made by judges when a dubious point calls for decision. Case law is thus built up as an attempt to fill the cracks in an *a priori* system. But any apparent realism in the concept of case law is frequently offset by the difficulty of linking two sets of circumstances in a way that satisfies both legal and real-life demands. Too often the legal link is a factual association, which to the client appears unrelated to the essential features of either case, e.g. A is alleged to have damaged someone else's property through carelessness which is character- istic of his behaviour and attitude; the only relevant legal prece- dent may lie in a case where B, a considerate and conscientious person, was found guilty of negligence for an isolated omission for which by common-sense standards he could not be held responsible. (A householder is not expected to spend his week- ends probing the wainscots on the off chance of finding damp wood in the vicinity of a neighbour's electric wiring.)

The volume of laws and precedents the practising lawyer is supposed to have at his finger-tips poses him with a daunting problem. The task of relating present circumstances to past judgements would be severe enough if clients could be trusted to speak clearly, consistently and relevantly. Some succeed in doing this, but many do not. Witnesses who are usually less involved in the outcome of a case than the client are at times even less reliable. Hence it is often hard for solicitor and barrister to form a convincing picture of the relevant facts. A barrister has the added responsibility of deciding how witnesses will stand up to cross examination; there would seem to be little or no correlation between the veracity of a witness and his performance in the box, and, veracity apart, it is far from easy to predict a witness' showing under stress. This holds for the testimony of expert witnesses as well as for ordinary citizens. The skilled advocate makes a study of a witness' foibles, his nervousness, his muddleheadedness, his susceptibility to flattery; indeed, the weaker his client's case, the stronger will be his incentive to exploit this kind of advantage. Great legal reputations have often been made by the advocate who can wring success from an apparently hopeless situation;

it may be easier to pursue a single desperate line of defence than to select from a plethora of favourable evidence. In the first type of case the scantiness of usable information may give lucidity and energy to its presentation.

Cases have to be built on facts rather than emotions, but the majority of clients do not resort to law until they have made protracted efforts to settle matters amicably. When they find that these efforts have failed, they may be suffering from a sense of cumulated grievance. To a client in this frame of mind his adviser's questions, sometimes asked for reasons not obvious to him, may result in his losing confidence in his legal representative's interest and integrity.

The gulf between law and life is accentuated by the rules and conventions governing court procedure; the questions that may or may not be asked, the sort of evidence that is admissible, the form of reply that is acceptable, the interventions of the judge, sometimes genuine attempts to straighten out the facts, at other times facetious, at others frankly biased. In addition there are the law's delays, which may result in the death or disappearance of key witnesses and distortions of memory among those who come forward. The summed effect of these happenings is at times to draw a veil over the initial circumstances, as though a world of conceptual unreality has been woven to take the place of the primary world of events. If it is asked how systems, devised by men of high ability and intelligence, can produce such bizarre distortions, the explanation is found to lie very largely in the limitations of individual memory and of the capacity for holding and handling information.

We are thus brought back by a long detour to the argument that concept formation is made necessary by the inability of the central nervous system to handle more than a limited amount of perceptual data. To extend experience beyond the events of the moment, it is necessary to abstract features common to events separated by time; to do this we must suppress the respects in which the events differ. This mechanism underlies the framing of all rules, regulations and laws, so that any body of laws must be a web of abstractions that takes account only of selected features in the individual situation. Any assumption that the particular set of circumstances with which a client is concerned will be treated in the court room as a unique happening is thus seen to be basically unsound. Hence the ambivalence with which so many citizens regard the law, which they venerate as an authority set up to protect them and distrust as a machinery whose toils must at all costs be avoided. It is known that many lawyers deplore these shortcomings, and considerable effort is being made to make the operation of English law more equitable and realistic.

No chapter on law and communication would be complete without reference to the manner in which legal documents are traditionally couched. Here is an example from the first piece of paper to hand, which happens to be the last lease of the present writer's house:

> 'Except and reserving nevertheless to the Lessors their and each of their executors administrators and assigns the free and uninterrupted passage of water and soil through the drains sewers and pipes and the free and uninterrupted use of all gaspipes waterpipes electric and other wires or other conducting media flues and drains which now are or may at any time hereafter be in on or passing through or under the said piece or parcel of land and premises hereby demised and any right of light or air or other easement over any adjoining or neighbouring property with power etc. etc. etc.'

The layman's disorientation in these verbal labyrinths would not be an argument against them if it could be shown that they assisted the processes of legal thinking, but how many of today's lawyers would be prepared to defend such an anti-style on these grounds?

29 Medicine

THE location of defects in an electronic system is frequently referred to as fault diagnosis. Without implying that the human organism resembles any system yet invented by ourselves, we may ask how far the adoption of this traditionally medical term is justified. The dictionary entry for diagnosis gives 'recognition' as the root meaning (from Greek via Latin), the main definition being 'Identification of disease by means of patient's symptoms'. The root meaning of symptom is 'falling' and its definition is 'Perceptible change in the body or its functions indicating disease'. Thus a symptom is a piece of evidence that the body has fallen from its customary state of equilibrium. A distinction is made between subjective symptoms, perceptible only to the patient, and objective symptoms which are perceptible to others.

A piece of equipment may cease to function or emit signs that it is likely to do so. The latter signs may be compared to the objective symptoms of a human patient, but fault diagnosis frequently implies system failure without preliminary warning. When this occurs there are no symptoms, unless total breakdown may be regarded as such. From this point the medical analogy wears thin, calling to mind the post mortem rather than any diagnosis for treatment.

This preamble suggests that the communication of subjective symptoms plays an essential role in most medical diagnoses. Even in routine examinations the doctor is to some degree dependent on the patient's answers, and in the majority of cases the patient takes the initiative in securing the examinations that result in treatment.

There are many problems in the communication of subjective symptoms. Leaving aside the obvious instances of the patient who won't stop talking and the doctor who won't start to listen, the difficulty of interpreting the patient's account in terms of the available objective signs has four main origins:

1) Some symptoms are typical of more than one condition.
2) Some conditions give rise to no subjective symptoms.
3) There is far from perfect correlation between the subjective and objective aspects of many symptoms.
4) Some patients have great difficulty in locating and describing their symptoms.

Ambiguous symptoms

Subjective symptoms may be ambiguous for purely verbal reasons, e.g. a patient may refer to many different conditions as headache or as backache. The doctor will press for more precise description: 'Is the pain sharp or dull? In the temples or at the back? Does it hurt when I press here?' One or two questions reinforced by appropriate prodding will usually make things clearer. The ambiguous objective symptom presents greater difficulty, especially when a cluster of several are met in more than one condition; above all when one of the conditions is common and the other encountered very rarely.

Absence of subjective symptoms

The obvious danger is that the disease will not be recognized till it has reached an advanced state. But the patient can hardly be held responsible for failing to communicate something he has had no hint of.

Lack of correlation between subjective and objective symptoms

Pain or discomfort are the main factors that send patients to the doctor, and sensitivity to either can vary enormously from one patient to another. One man's pain perception can be so low that he has no warning when his tissues are being burned or crushed (though admittedly this is a pathological condition), others suffer acutely from organically trivial causes. One of the doctor's problems is to distinguish the latter type of case from a psychogenic reaction, a distinction not always successfully achieved.

Patients' difficulties in describing their symptoms

This may result from verbal brashness ('Doctor, it's agonizing,' 'Actually I'm not feeling too good') or defective body-imagery (the point of felt discomfort giving no clue to the source of damage).

Many doctors in England have found it hard to adapt to the conditions of the last twenty years. To a lot the Health Service has meant crowded waiting-rooms, vast increases in the demand for prescriptions and certificates of absence, and ever more copious intakes of pharmaceutical literature. It is hard in such circumstances to discriminate the more from the less deserving cases, and to give the former the individual attention they need.

The patient too has his problems. While many still defer uncritically to medical authority and are ready to assume that whatever is done (or not done) is for the best, others, more intelligent and often with a long history of indifferent health, find it impossible to be so acquiescent. These people expect considered answers to their questions and resent being fobbed off with bromide phrases and facetious shrugs. The chronic sufferer, aware that no cure has been found for his complaint but obliged to seek palliatives for his growing disabilities, is sometimes made to feel that the persistence of his ailment has become an offence and that his desire to live a positive life in spite of it is meeting with scant sympathy. Doctors who have enjoyed robust health sometimes lack the imagination to grasp the conditions under which their patients have to face living. This lack of sensitivity can be communicated all too readily, sometimes by an untimely phrase, sometimes by no more than an irritated glance. There are circumstances where understanding can have a tonic effect even where the skill to cure is defective.

Some forms of psychiatric treatment (interview therapy and above all psycho-analysis) are in essence subtilized techniques of communication. Here the psychiatrist has to perform the delicate task of entering into a dynamic relationship with the patient and at the same time maintaining his detachment. If he becomes too involved in the situation, his perception and judgement are likely to suffer and he will become prey to emotional exhaustion. If he remains aloof or allows his attention to relax, his patient becomes immediately aware of his shift in attitude.

Neurotic patients are likely to make keen demands, and the business of resisting such demands without alienating confidence calls for continuous skill and alertness.

It is likely that the roles of doctor and patient will undergo a transformation comparable to that already developing between teacher and pupil. In the past physicians and schoolmasters have been invested with an authority relatively immune from challenge. Today their authority must be underwritten by a demonstrable competence, a readiness to meet pupil and patient on their own ground and if necessary to admit ignorance. In this way the status of pupil and patient will be gradually raised from one of unquestioning obedience to one of contributory effort.

30　Scientific research

THE relation between everyday ('literary') and scientific language is a difficult issue which no writer on communication can evade. These pages contain several protests against the sharp dichotomy which represents ordinary language as vague and diffuse and scientific language as precise and unambiguous. It is argued that the real distinction is between the language of open and closed systems, and urged that the language of scientists cannot be assigned exclusively to the latter. The advance of science may be viewed as the setting up and testing of an endless succession of models, each conceived initially to throw light on a limited range of phenomena. In postulating a particular model, it is necessary to assign fixity of meaning to its key terms, i.e. to treat the model as a closed system. The training of scientists consists very largely in preparation for this exacting task, and the greater part of most scientists' working life is devoted to operating within this kind of context. Such training and practice throw emphasis on the need for rigorous analysis, and engender distrust and suspicion of every kind of inexact statement. This leads to an attitude which some-times fails to distinguish the imprecise from the imaginative, and which is apt to overlook the origins of many scientifically fruitful concepts. When we penetrate the esoteric surface of many technical terms, we usually come upon an image of unexpected concreteness and simplicity. This surely is evidence that our most radical thinking is the product of immediate experience, a fact that can long be hidden from us when we are working out the implications of some well-established line of thought or tech-nique.

It is salutary to turn to the writings of an accredited expert like William Whewell (32) who, more than a century ago, recognized and tackled another crisis of scientific information. Sensing that a linguistic babel was dissipating the research findings of his generation, he set out to supply 'rules which may tend to preserve the purity of scientific language from wanton and needless violation'. The rules he evolved are remarkable for their common sense and their refusal to subscribe to any dogmatic extremism. Thus he argued that the 'appropriation of old words was preferable to the invention of new' and that 'when common words were appropriated as technical terms, their meaning in common use should be retained as far as convenient'. A purist might reply that to adopt common words for technical usage is to invite misunderstanding, and no doubt there is a limited truth in this. Whewell saw that it is better to take a limited risk of this kind than to set up scientific activity as a priestly mystery remote from the affairs of human beings. To do the latter might bring its practitioners immediate prestige and wealth, but would tend in the long run to establish a sterile cult. It may be added that Whewell's advice was sought by many leading scientists including Faraday, who adopted the terms anode and cathode on his advice but drew the line at his suggestion that Faraday's kind should be known as physicists. Other terms owed to Whewell include eocene, miocene and pliocene, and, most comprehensive of all, scientist. 'As an Artist is a Musician, Painter or Poet, a Scientist is a Mathematician, Physicist or Naturalist.'

While a scientist approaches his problems analytically and without prejudice, he has to make assumptions before he embarks on research. Some of these assumptions are necessary to his thinking but incapable of demonstration; so far as they cannot be demonstrated they must be seen as acts of faith. The point is forcefully put in a review printed in the *Scientific American** of two recent works by eminent physicists:

'Modern physics prides itself on having swept away most of the metaphysics that was long considered essential to any scientific discipline. It has, of course, achieved no such emancipation, having simply substituted a new metaphysic for an old one. Indeed, it would probably be impossible to conduct a meaningful physical discourse and to handle the abstractions, symbols and logical transformations that are characteristic of the transactions of physics if certain underlying metaphysical assumptions were not accepted

—even if these assumptions are not acknowledged. One has only to look at these two books that attempt to explain the character of modern physics to the non-specialist to realize what a formidable structure of metaphysical theories forms the underpinning of the discipline. Oppenheimer's three short lectures are concerned with space and time, atom and field, and a somewhat general evaluation of the relation between science and politics. The lectures are more successful in creating a mood, or perhaps one might say a poetic picture, of modern physics than in elucidating its concepts. The performance is not without virtuosity; one can be reasonably sure that the audience experienced intellectual exhilaration even not complete enlightenment.

'Park's book is a fuller, more systematic popularization of such topics as the properties of nuclei, quantum mechanics, gravity, elementary particles, symmetry and the like. He begins his account skillfully and carries the reader a good way in showing how the modern ideas of physics evolved. But after a time the story bogs down in complexities, qualifications, subqualifications, dilemmas, paradoxes and puzzles—all of which are the notorious attendants of this sophisticated, fascinating and infuriatingly difficult science. There is the pretense that the propositions of physics pertain to "real" entities in the physical world, and there is also the pretense that there are properties of physics so abstract that although one can make use of them one must not inquire too closely into their meaning in terms of physical reality. That both of these pretenses have substance and are necessary to the pursuit of physics is the best evidence of its elaborate metaphysical apparatus.'

Scientific American, June 1965

What is said here of physics is applicable to some extent to other disciplines. However rigorously a scientist may make use of his chosen model, the model itself will bear the marks of undemonstrable assumptions. Hence a major difficulty in communicating the full implications of scientific research lies in the fact that assumptions necessary to the scientist's mental processes may play no part in the layman's. This is a sophisticated instance of the barrier that has been termed incompatibility of schemas. The more obvious linguistic barriers, the employment of words whose meaning is obscure to the untrained, can to some extent be removed by explanation and definition. This assumes, of course, that the reader or listener is broadly aware of general scientific intentions, aware that the scientist is concerned to observe accurately, to generate hypotheses for experimental verification, and that his goals are related to some form of systematic prediction. If these objectives are not understood, communication on more specific matters can hardly be successful.

The reviewer's comment on the probable reaction of Oppenheimer's audience merits brief attention. To say that an audience experiences exhilaration rather than enlightenment suggests a failure by the lecturer to convey any part of his intentions. It may be doubted if his failure was as complete as that. To some the creation of a mood or even a poetic picture can serve as a gateway to later comprehension, perhaps even of an intuitive grasp of a subject's range and goals. To write this off as an ephemeral state of emotion is to ignore the part played by intuition in creative science. Rigorous analysis and quantification are the tools of science rather than its source. Many major discoveries have originated not in logic or calculation but in imagery, as though a working model of a baffling problem had appeared in fantasy before the inquirer. If this is true of the genesis of great projects, it is rash to dismiss all imaginative presentation as bogus.

Few scientists today regard popular writing as an unworthy occupation. The need for a more general dissemination of scientific ideas and findings is all apparent and many high quality texts have been produced in response to it. Some texts alleged to be for the benefit of laymen and first-year students make one wonder how the author would set about addressing his peers. The hint of an answer may perhaps be found by comparing the styles of presentation of a long-established scientific journal such as *Nature* and a more recent production like the *New Scientist*. It will be obvious that they are designed to serve different purposes, both important and necessary. But the distinction is not between scientific and non-scientific readership; it is rather between specific and general scientific reading. It would be interesting to know how many are equipped to assimilate all the sections of *Nature*'s correspondence columns and how many scientists turn to the more recent publication for guidance on topics outside their own discipline.

Failures of communication between members of different sciences and even those of the same are by no means unusual. Here it should be possible to assume that all, whatever their subject matter, are agreed on broad objectives and share the same method-ological principles. What, then, are the sources of misunder-standing?

1) Each discipline develops its own vocabulary and there is no reason why the meaning of the more specific terms used by a physicist should be self-evident to a botanist or a biologist. It is possible that more might be done to develop a Basic Scientific English, but new terms are continually being brought into use and no complete solution to this difficulty seems possible. The most serious barrier is not the unfamiliar word (which merely delays understanding) but the common term where variations in connotation can escape detection.

2) The subject matter of each discipline poses special problems in evaluation and these are reflected in extensions of the basic mathe-matical techniques and the development of new ones. Thus the statistics employed by a sociologist may be unfamiliar to a biologist and vice versa.

3) The nature of the subject matter also influences the nature of experimental work, or at times, as with astronomy, precludes experiment altogether. There is a particularly strong contrast between the methods of the physical sciences (where a very high degree of control and measurement precision are possible) and most types of field research in the social sciences.

4) An added complication in psychology is the existence of the sub-science of individual differences, which stems from the scientist's special relationship with his subject matter (regard for the individual human being as person) and also from the high degree of plasticity in human behaviour.

5) A major contemporary difficulty arises from the vast amount of research in progress and the increasing tempo of discovery and conceptual reformulation. This means not only that knowledge quickly becomes obsolete, but that its providers tend to become obsolete too. It is not merely that facts are continuously added to the scientific granary, but that basic thinking undergoes continuous change. Thus a man who graduated in physics or chemistry ten years ago may already be out of contact with the student of today. The phenomenon of basic theory altering several times in the course of a scientist's working life must, to put it mildly, offer problems in adjustment. The old assumption that a scientist could devote his intellectual life to working out ideas conceived in youth appears to have lost its validity. Similarly, the notion that the senior scientist's role is to instruct and super-

vise his juniors must today be balanced by his need to learn from them. Once again one-way communication is yielding to two-way transaction.

A final difficulty concerns the thinker unable to make his intuitions effective in the state of existing knowledge. Such a person is denied intellectual rapport with his own generation or anyway with those elements in it he is most anxious to appeal to. His ideas will be dismissed by his contemporaries as nonsensical because they cannot find expression in the language of the day. This sort of thing is familiar enough at a humbler level. A child of six cannot operate mentally on the plane of a child of ten, nor can a child of ten on the level of a fifteen-year-old. The effect of this is that a communication characteristic of a mature intelligence will be dismissed as meaningless by one less mature, or else will be rendered down to a point where only casual features are recognizable. The reception of advanced ideas by more conservative intelligences sometimes entails a similar travesty.

31 Creative art

APART possibly from criticism, all the activities so far discussed are directed to specific ends in terms of which their utility or lack of it can be assessed. Creative art is not specific in this sense, though well-meaning people persist in treating it as though it were. 'Where can we fit these people in?' they ask. 'How can their work be given significance?' This philanthropy leaves out of account that many artists regard their work less as a luxury than an inescapable necessity. To ignore this paradox, to think of art as a skill to be manipulated by others for the good of the community, is to confuse a way of life with an activity. If we must talk of significance in their connection, two things should be said: first, that people of this type appear to have existed in all societies; secondly, that many of them enjoy a kind of Cassandra relationship with their environment—that is, while seeming to reject what it stands for, they are none the less unusually alert to its trends, their pre-awareness casting them for the sort of role Jung assigned to the unconscious. As the individual's unconscious is said to act as compensator to the excesses of consciousness, the artist flashes a stream of warnings to society.

It is not possible to produce experimental evidence for statements of the above kind; they are based on observations and inductions it is impossible to quantify. And there are numerous exceptions. The point is made, in spite of all the evidence that may seem to conflict with it, to place the role of the artist in a proper relation to other roles.

Another unfortunate tendency is found in efforts to equate artistic activity with psychic abnormality. There seem to be several factors behind this aberration. First, it has been noted that many artists profess indifference to the goals that structure the life patterns of others, e.g. to wealth, power and social position. So far as this is a valid generalization, the explanation lies in a powerful motive incompatible with the pursuit of other motives. But this is not a peculiarity of artists; it is true of pioneers of every kind, whether their activity is science, chess, scholarship, mountaineering or social reform. A second reason lies in the therapeutic value of art in some instances of mental disturbance; from this the illicit inference is made that the practice of art is at all times a defence against psychic disorder, so that those who devote their lives to it are engaged in a continual struggle with the forces of disintegration. Thirdly is the fact that tension is often a condition of creativity, so that the life of an artist may show an unusual oscillation in this respect, peaks of high tension alternating with depths of detension. To many people high tension spells nervous imbalance and the idea that some accept it, live with it and turn it to account appears almost a perversion. Fourthly, there is the question of how far the artist's personal life is related to his work. The answer to this is apt to seem two-faced. If we say that work is detached and objectified, this can be taken to deny any influence from daily activity; if we say that it contains autobiographical elements, this appears to refute the idea of detachment. Yet both are true. A work of art is objective in the sense that it is complete in itself and its impact is not dependent on any knowledge of the forces that have given rise to it; it is autobiographical or anyway autopsychological in the sense that had the circumstances of the artist's life been different, his work would have reflected those differences. It is, however, usually profitless to try and deduce the artist's condition from his work, one reason being that there is no certain way of distinguishing the life of fantasy from the life of reality. Finally, the artist's medium of communication is his art, and while there are artists highly articulate in other media, there are many who are not. It is therefore not to be wondered at that some are uncommunicative under questioning, in this resembling the mathematician who, coaxed to utterance by a persistent interviewer, could only articulate the words 'Mathematics is a language'.

There are specific aspects of aesthetic communication that lend themselves more readily to quantification. Every art entails specialization in one or more sensory modality in each of which a number of components can be discriminated, e.g. musical sound requires perception of pitch, tempo, volume, rhythm; pictorial art of colour, tone value, balance, design and so on.

Tests to measure these varieties of discrimination have long existed and they make a useful contribution. It is of value to know how far these aspects of perception intercorrelate and to be able to draw attention to a weakness in an aspirant's armoury. But it would be unrealistic to pretend that such instruments take us a very long way in deciding who will develop the keenest sensibility, let alone those likely to express themselves creatively through a medium. Such questions entail a great complexity of factors over and above the possession of discriminatory powers. In view of this, the question 'How does the artist communicate with the recipient?' can best be attacked by inserting probes at a number of selected points.

First, then, there is no reason why the recipient should retrace the artist's creative path; indeed it is usually regarded as a sign of mastery if a work of art appears inevitable, as if it has achieved the only possible form. So far as it does this it will conceal that the artist underwent any doubts or questioning in producing it.

Most art media arouse pleasure in themselves. This pleasure is distinct from that aroused by the individual work, but it is likely to exert some influence on the recipient's mental set. This influence will have an affective tinge.

The early stages of most narratives and dramas supply the recipient with material necessary to an understanding of what follows. In addition, the development of plot is normally in terms of cause and effect. Both of these are addressed to cognition. The plan or layout of many art forms is dominated by requirements that dictate the form of an intellectual communication. Common features include the statement of one or more themes and the themes' development in the light of the implications unfolded.

Although the purpose of a well-presented argument is to demonstrate and convince, it often excites pleasure and admiration for itself. Such attitudes are often termed aesthetic; indeed it is possible to adopt such an attitude to almost any object. This, however, does not make the objects works of art in any but a figurative sense.

An aesthetic experience must be defined in terms of attitude rather than mechanism. The attitude adopted is a complex of detachment and involvement; detached in the sense that the recipient accepts the work as an end in itself, involved in that the experience commands attention and excites emotion. There is no evidence that any special mechanisms of perception or affect are called into play.

It is usual to ascribe to major artists a high degree of inventiveness, intellectual power and the capacity to excite strong affect. Inventiveness refers to fecundity of ideas, and, more subtly, to the ability to present a given idea in many ways, to wring a maximum of variation and development from a theme. Intellectual power shows itself mainly in an ability to organize and give direction to a wide range of material. The power of exciting affect can be exercised in more than one way; with some recipients it is stirred automatically by the exercise of invention and intellect, with others it is enhanced if the work is felt to be based on some human experience whose significance it enhances.

The great artist is sometimes said to express the spirit of his time, an assertion that raises more questions than it answers. While some artists come to fame on the crest of a wave they have helped to propagate, there are others whose work seems posthumously to have been in advance of the period it was produced in. Two comments are possible. First, an important artist must be in vital contact with something, but the nature of this something must be very liberally interpreted so as to include themes as far apart as the aspirations of a repressed people and the artist's personal conflicts. Secondly, it will be easier for an artist whose outlook and choice of theme are in line with the contemporary climate of opinion to achieve recognition. The artist whose views are out of line may fail to win a public, but this is not necessarily due to any shortcomings in his work.

The effect of art is to extend the boundaries of consciousness by giving expression to what has hitherto eluded it. Until an experience has been expressed, it may be regarded as inexpressible by all except the artist. There is an analogy here with the scientist concerned to solve a difficult problem. Such a problem may be insoluble in terms of any existing model; it will then be declared beyond the scope of scientific methodology. Up till a hundred and fifty years ago this was the accepted view of the full range of psychological problems. It is still said of many human issues. The scientist preoccupied with such a theme may be compelled to forge a new scientific model, just as the artist in a similar predicament has to forge a new technique.

The time taken to assimilate a factual statement is measurable, though it may appear without duration to introspection; the time required to follow a coherent argument is to all intents and purposes the time required to read or hear it. But a work of art that gives up its total meaning by the end of one perusal or performance is generally a shallow one. As a rule first performance sets up something analogous to a persistent after-image in the recipient, as though a seed has been planted and must grow and run its cycle. This need for temporal development is bound up with the fact that the presentation evokes more than a thought or a mood; these could be elicited with no basic adjustment of perception, which is what originality appears to demand.

A work of art can mean different things to the same recipient on different occasions. This appears to be a function of condensation, a mechanism which enables the artist (like the dreamer) to concentrate different levels of meaning into the same text. To take an obvious example: *Hamlet* can be accepted as melodrama by a playgoer whose taste favours this, but the playgoer with an ear for undertone hears something totally different; each interpretation is complete in itself, the two dramas coexisting in a single text. The parallelism of esoteric and exoteric readings attributed to much scriptural writing is a similar instance of condensation. A special form of this mechanism consists in the juxtaposition of elements from different levels of experience. 'And Jacob was left alone; and there wrestled a man with him till the breaking of the day.'

Ambiguity which, as Empson has pointed out, can be a major poetic weapon, is a close relative of condensation. Whereas condensation permits the recipient to select an interpretation appropriate to his level of understanding, ambiguity enhances the pleasure of the sophisticated.

Redundancy is a yet more potent instrument. Most of the means by which the poet gains his effects contain some lacing of it—alliteration, assonance, rhyme, metre. Similarly with the plastic arts, where words like colour scheme, interchange, pattern imply the repetition of selected shapes and tones as a source of gratification. The redundancy favoured by verbal artists rarely consists of sheer repetition; usually it involves the selection and patterning of a few favoured elements, at times building up to a powerful consonantal barrage:

'A beetling baldbright cloud thorough England
Riding: there did storms not mingle? and
Hailropes hustle and grind their
Heavengravel? wolfsnow, worlds of it, wind there?'

In factual communication redundancy is held to be wasteful and slackening beyond the point where it is necessary to ensure understanding. It is of interest to find a factor accorded scant respect in the intellectual world raised to the level of a creative instrument in a work of imagination.

A great deal of failure in communication has been ascribed to schema incompatibility between sender and receiver. The human being interprets the external world in terms of the schemas which various influences have established in him. When he encounters the work of someone whose schemas resemble his own, understanding is easily set up; when the divergence is great, communication is made difficult. It seems probable that likes and dislikes are closely related to ease or difficulty of communication; and, so far as this is so, it points to schema incompatibility as the source of divergent response.

This chapter has been concerned with communication between artist and audience or spectator; it has hardly touched the yet more complex issue of the artist's self-communication. This area has received little illumination from professional psychologists, who have at times resisted enlightenment from other quarters. For example, Koestler's *Act of Creation* (62), though published with an enthusiastic foreword from Burt, has not yet received the attention it merits. The book sets out a wealth of evidence from three major fields of mental activity. To the criticism that the author has carried out no experimentation of his own, the answer must be that the insight of an imaginative writer should prove invaluable in devising experimental strategies in so rich and difficult a field. It is one thing to study creativity at the level of simple problem-solving, another to ask questions relevant to the activities of Kepler and Michelangelo. While it is right to press experimental activity forward wherever it has the least chance of succeeding, it is useless to boycott areas where present chances seem remote but where understanding can be enlarged by theory and example.

32 Personal relationships

'Communication is too alarming. To enter into someone else's life is too frightening. To disclose to others the poverty within us is too fearsome a possibility.'

Harold Pinter

Fear of self-disclosure is only one of the hazards that discourage intimacy; fear of exposing oneself to excessive emotional demand is for some an equally powerful deterrent. But to present the issue in a balanced way we should add that many experience an overwhelming need for intimacy, a need that can only be crushed at enormous cost. Further, whatever the humiliations and exasperations risked in the search for close personal relationship, there is no support for the view that mutually rewarding intimacy is a figment of the adolescent mind. Such intimacies are realized from time to time, even if they do not supply much nourishment for drama. But it would be over-ambitious to try to subject such phenomena to experimental study, and having said this we must be satisfied to discuss this chapter's theme at a more modest level.

This book is concerned with the types of message one individual wishes to transmit to another, the barriers that distort or prevent transmission, and the lines of research relevant to these problems. The basic questions are: how shall A ensure that B understands what A sets out to convey? or, where the message contains an affective element: how can A ensure that the appropriate affective state is aroused? We are interested in the mechanics rather than the motives behind a communication. It is not our purpose to ask whether A's intention is to transmit information for its own sake or whether he wishes to persuade, manipulate or exploit his hearer. These are admittedly highly important questions, but an attempt to outline the main areas of human communication cannot do more than draw attention to such possibilities. It is, however, necessary to point to two more basic qualifications. The situation between sender and receiver must be differentiated to the point of asking whether A and B are encountering one another as individual persons or as the occupants of assigned roles; and, a wider question still, whether communication between them is facilitated or retarded by the interaction of their personalities.

The concept of role has received considerable attention from sociologists and social psychologists, largely in connection with the place of individuals in formal organizations and the need for clear definition of function. Such need originates frequently in the practical necessity of dividing work and responsibility. In the simplest instance, the volume of work falling to one person may increase to a point where division between two or more people becomes called for. This may or may not entail a division of function. If the function is unchanged, we find two people working where one worked before, each being able to ask and answer the questions to which the work gives rise. With a functional division, the position is somewhat different; we find X speaking for his half of the work and Y speaking for his. From time to time X will be heard saying, 'This should be referred to Y' or 'This is Y's pigeon', and he will develop a skill for examining new work in terms of its X-relevance. He may, particularly if he is a man of marked ability, come to be endowed with a plurality of roles; he may then be heard saying, 'Wearing my X hat I see it this way, but if I put on my Z hat it looks like this.' There is a limit to the number of roles a man can assume and clearly no two roles must involve undue contradiction; a lawyer cannot prosecute and defend in the same action, a banker gets confused if he borrows too freely from himself. A man's words will be influenced by whether he is assuming a role or not, as when a commanding officer reprimands a subordinate for a spirited but irregular piece of behaviour and follows his rebuke with muted personal congratulations. To the uninitiated, perception of the roles assumed by others often occasions bewilderment, while to the sophisticated the naïve man's inability to assume a role may afford exasperation and embarrassment.

Attention to the importance of defining formal roles may well have made us all more conscious of the less formal kind we have always taken for granted. There is a quickened awareness of the self as child, parent, spouse, employer, householder and so on which makes the individual less ready to become identified with a single dominant role. The absolutism of earlier attitudes (I am a father and I demand the respect proper to one) has given way to a self-conscious relativism (I may be a father, but I remember what it is to be a child). If the danger of absolutism is to identify the role with the self, that of relativism may be to lose sight of the self behind a cinerama of phantom images. Some people today share the dilemma of the Pirandello character who exclaims, 'I am this to this man, that to that man, but when all is said and done, what am I to myself?' It is probable that someone sometime has set out to demonstrate that a man is the sum of all the roles he has ever assumed, and that when these have been systematically discarded no identity remains. (Despite his title, Erving Goffman (40) sometimes comes near to this position in his *Presentation of Self in Everyday Life*.) Without entering on a round of metaphysical speculation, we may draw attention to what happens when the same role is enacted by half a dozen persons in turn, when, for example, each member of a small group assumes the position of chairman in a committee exercise. Here, with role held constant, it is customary to remark on the range of personality displayed and the reflection of this in the variety of ways in which the same duties can be performed.

To what extent does personality facilitate or retard communication? This question can be considered from the point of view of the sender in isolation, and from that of the sender in relation to different receivers. The personality of the sender may influence his preference of medium, his perception of a receiver's attitudes and the extent to which he is inclined to make communications at all. The main communicating media are speech and writing, and there are occasions appropriate to each. The man who writes rather than speaks is apt to set up barriers which personal contact could often avoid; the man who distrusts paper leaves no record of his decisions and actions, which in many circumstances are important to ensure continuity and the resumption of argument at a later date.

It has been said of two British Prime Ministers that one possessed no antennae, while the other possessed nothing else. If by antennae we understand alertness to nuance and undertone, it is easy to see how either tendency can lead to failure in business and government. The man who is all perception is likely to reflect the prevailing mood without adding direction of his own; the leader deaf to the moods and feelings of others may produce clear-cut plans, but will be unable to gauge their acceptability.

If personality affects the choice of media by the sender, it follows that sharp resemblances or dissimilarities of personality will influence the flow of information between sender and receiver. We must not, however, jump to the conclusion that close similarity of mood and tempo offer the ideal condition for partnership. It may be true that communication is an impossibility between those who figuratively speak different languages, but observation suggests that successful partnership—in business, on the stage, in politics, in marriage—is often marked by personality contrast. Extremes of likeness and unlikeness may each inhibit sympathetic understanding; the individual in search of a collaborator no more needs a replica of himself than an opposite with whom he has nothing in common. This hypothesis appears to be supported by one of the few experimental studies bearing on the issue. In a study of the ability to communicate emotional meaning it was noted that high interpersonal compatibility was associated with a moderately high perceptiveness between sender and receiver, whereas low compatibility was associated with high as well as low perceptiveness of the partner's efforts to convey this type of meaning.

It is sometimes noted that persons meeting for the first time appear to enter into an immediate *rapport*, while persistent attempts at communication by the well-intentioned often lead nowhere. To some extent, likes and dislikes seem to be rooted in physical and chemical affinities communicated without conscious effort. If such affinities are very strong, they may induce a belief in compatibility at other levels, e.g. sexual attraction can masquerade as intellectual and emotional harmony. While many hope for and some attain a relationship which fuses all the main dimensions of personality, there are numerous instances of intimacy along a single dimension, intellectual companionship without emotional complication, affective compatibility between those of widely separated intellectual interests, sexual *rapport* without mental or affective sympathy.

33 Is any experience essentially incommunicable?

'It is the function of art to express the inexpressible.'

Goethe

'There is indeed the inexpressible. This *shows* itself; it is the mystical.

'The right method of philosophy would be this. To say nothing except what can be said, i.e. the propositions of natural science, i.e. something that has nothing to do with philosophy: and then always, when someone else wished to say something metaphysical, to demonstrate to him that he had given no meaning to certain signs in his propositions. This method would be unsatisfying to the other—he would not have the feeling that we were teaching him philosophy—but it would be the only strictly correct method.

'My propositions are elucidatory in this way: he who understands me finally recognizes them as senseless, when he has climbed out through them, on them, over them. (He must so to speak throw away the ladder, after he has climbed up on it.)

'He must surmount these propositions; then he sees the world rightly.

'Whereof one cannot speak, thereof one must be silent.'

Wittgenstein

The famous last words of the *Tractatus* offer as good an approach as we shall find to the question of communicability. On the face of it Wittgenstein's book is a contradiction of his main thesis, which is, put crudely, that communication is only possible when there is perfect correspondence between expression and its object. Such correspondence, he asserts, is to be found in the propositions of natural science and nowhere else. Propositions of this kind deal with facts, and facts are public coin about which it is possible to speak with total clarity and freedom from ambiguity, proof of which lies in the possibility of basing predictions on factual propositions and verifying them later. It would not be possible to do this if the proposition meant one thing to one man and something else to another, which in Wittgenstein's view is equivalent to saying that it does not mean anything at all. But works of philosophy do not carry a single unequivocal meaning to every reader, nor can we base experiments directly upon them. Hence Wittgenstein, a philosopher of scientific method, seems to be denying that his own work can communicate. Even his greatest admirers have found this hard to accept.

How deep is the contradiction? Is it more than a verbal confusion? We commonly use the word communicate both of messages that transmit confirmable information ('The thermometer on my wall registers 64° Fahrenheit') and of those that try to convey our own states of feeling and mind ('I am too hot', 'I am worried about the state of the world'). The first of these is often referred to as objective statement, the second as subjective. If someone says 'I intend to use communicate only of objective statements because these are the only statements that can be transmitted without ambiguity', he is entitled to his convention. Is this what Wittgenstein is trying to say? He certainly is saying this, but he goes much further for he adds that if one cannot speak unambiguously, one should not speak at all. The implication is that the urge to speak, the need to create new meaning is suspect, even though it is this urge that leads people like himself to speak and write. Such an implication is essentially anti-psychological, for it denies the validity of everything that makes human communication possible. If we take Wittgenstein at face value, he is saying not merely that all affective messages are incommunicable but that most content messages are too, since even these carry a penumbra of subjectivity. The only messages that conform fully to his prescription are sign messages, and these do so because signs are conventions devoid of connotation.

It need hardly be said that sign messages and the codes on which they are based are the product of a highly sophisticated intellectuality. So also are conceptual and scientific ways of thinking, which up to a point have much in common with codes. Conceptual thinking aims to be free of the individual moment or event, aspiring always to higher levels of abstraction. But sign messages, though free of association with any particular occasion (an 'a' transmitted on Monday is no different from an 'a' transmitted on Sunday), cannot be said to aspire at all. They amount to mechanical transactions in an accepted currency. They represent the elements through which meaning can be expressed, but they themselves express nothing. Alter the code—use 'b' where you used 'z' and 'q' where you used 'j'—and another run of transactions becomes possible. The code is wholly arbitrary; all that is necessary for it to work is agreement about what signs correspond to what sounds; there is no sense in which the sign expresses the sound (if it did so once, all that is long forgotten.)

The view of mind as an instrument which, used rightly, can give totally objective information is rooted in the fallacy that mind is a passive recorder of external information. We argued earlier that this was a layman's error, that perception is an interactive process, a transaction between brain and environment. The notion of non-participant observation is thus a sophisticated version of an unsophisticated assumption, at variance with the view of the brain as an adaptive organ, an instrument that is continually revising its perceptions and its concepts. It is not, of course, denied that training can sharpen and refine our mental processes and so make us capable of objectivity within the limits of our development; this can create the illusion of an absolute objectivity which may go unchallenged for a long time. But in the end a limit will be reached, our approved models will yield diminishing returns, and new problems will remain unsolved till a basic revision in conceptual thinking is brought about. The mechanism which makes such revision possible cannot be accounted for in conscious terms; it appears to entail a regression to fantasy levels. How consciousness can be reactivated by a surrender to more primitive modes of experience will perhaps appear contradictory to those who draw a hard-and-fast line between imagination and intellect. But such distinctions, though useful in discussion, lead to a sterile dualism if pressed too far.

The position we are moving to is that sharp dichotomous thinking (subjective versus objective, communication versus non-communication) has been prompted by dialectical necessity rather than the facts of existence. The view that communication is of an all-or-nothing kind, that the slightest tincture of imprecision annihilates the message transmitted has no warrant in reality. We communicate with greater or less effectiveness, sometimes our efforts give rise to catastrophic misunderstanding, we meet people who appear to be on a totally different wavelength from ourselves; the effects of all these happenings can be deeply disturbing, but they do not lend force to the belief that any experience is essentially unconveyable.

Admittedly some experiences are harder to transmit than others. The complex intellectual experience depends for its reception on a certain level of mental ability reinforced by training and a background state of information; to the extent that these are lacking in the recipient, the message will be received in a partial form. The affective experience which may result from a sequence of events spread over many years will be yet more difficult to convey. Here we must accept that the experience in all its details is likely to remain private, but there is no reason why its essential features may not be perceived and shared by an imaginative recipient or by one who has undergone a similar ordeal. In addition, the signs of such experiences can often be recognized by a trained observer, who may or may not be capable of entering into the quality of the condition. Whether both these types of transmission should be rated communication depends on the purpose of the sender. If his aim is to arouse understanding or sympathy he will not be satisfied by a diagnosis, however accurate; if he requires alleviation, it will not matter to him whether his physician has suffered migraine or insomnia.

The problem of communicability reaches its climax with the extreme experience. Among the forms this may take we may mention crippling personal loss, sharp reversal of fortune, the infliction of injustice, a thunderbolt love affair, the lightning flash of mystical experience. These events frequently produce a compulsion to communicate coupled with the conviction that communication can never be achieved. The latter may perhaps be rooted in the sense that the subject has become alienated from his past life, so that he cannot make contact with the person he used to be. This would explain why it tends to be the communicator who stresses the inefficacy of words at the same time as he wrestles with them to forge new messages. It is possible that some such dissonance was at work in Wittgenstein, manifesting itself in the contradictions we began by noticing; it may even be that the tension between two personalities, as though Russell and the prophet Isaiah were struggling to possess the same psyche, conferred a significance upon his writing which we do not find in the lucid consistency of more temperate expositors.

By contrast, Goethe's paradox attains its goal with effortless directness. Implicit in his statement are the assumptions that the human being is in dynamic contact with his environment, that he has evolved to the point of self-consciousness, that he feels a need to transmit the contents of consciousness, and that through the genius of a minority of gifted individuals he has found the means of doing so. At the same time, the uncommunicated remains uncommunicable until the territory of consciousness has been extended yet further. We accept Goethe's defiant paradox as a mechanism for bringing two levels of experience into relation. We boggle at Wittgenstein because he uses the language of one to repudiate the other. Drawing an uncompromising line between facts (of which the world is composed) and the world as a whole, he limits the possibility of communication to the first. Only propositions can be spoken and they deal with facts. 'What can be said at all can be said clearly', but 'The feeling of the world as a limited whole is the mystical feeling'. The 'said clearly' is apparently intended to restrict utterance to a single level of discourse, and this restriction is precisely what all imaginative writers refuse to be bound by and which Wittgenstein himself refuses to be bound by. The restriction is unexceptionable as long as the speaker is working out the implications of a stated model or logical system, which is what the majority of mathematicians and scientists spend their time doing. But as soon as the limits of the system have been reached, such a restriction leaves the thinker helpless, unable to extend his thinking and his experimental concepts. By this criterion Goethe's statement, a wilful contradiction, is 'unclear'. In fact it enlarges understanding. The capacity to do this is at the root of all creative thinking, including creative scientific thinking. If we deny this we are saying that all metaphor and analogy make for confusion, but if we consider the root meaning of key scientific concepts we find that nearly all of them have this type of origin. For confirmation we need look no further than the word entropy applied initially to a thermodynamic state and subsequently by analogy to the world of man-made communication.

PART FOUR

Communication as an Area of Psychological Research

34 Scientific method as an evolutionary process

SCIENTIFIC thinking developed against a background of religious belief, and many have seen this phase as a contest between the forces of enlightenment and obscurantism. Such people fail to notice that to a great extent a new set of beliefs has been substituted for an old one, and that often the new beliefs are held with the same dogmatism as those they have superseded. While much remains to be discovered about the way beliefs are formed and held, it is possible to make a few very general remarks. We may think of a belief as a mental habit, the residue of an attitude acquired in the first place by learning. Seen this way it represents an adjustment to some aspect of the environment and it will be clear that in this sense all human activities are dependent on beliefs which provide a stable platform from which to operate. The need for such stability is experienced whatever we do, whether we are executing a psychomotor activity or solving an intellectual problem. In every context the most successful habits are those that can go longest unchallenged; but belief passes into dogma when its holder behaves as though challenge is unthinkable. When this stage is reached, the human being is in danger of losing his powers of perception and adaptation. He has become imprisoned by habit, unable to react to new types of change, unable to learn. In the final stage he will repress all evidence of change, seeking to exist as though he were living in the past; in an intermediate phase he may become highly subjective, seeing and resenting change in everything.

The original worker in any field appears to most of his contemporaries as a destroyer who trades in novelty for its own sake. Years later when his innovations have been assimilated, he comes to be seen as one who has selected and discarded with ruthless insight, and who in doing so has incorporated whatever had survival value in the work of his predecessors. This implies that all lines of human activity must be viewed as evolving processes marked by moments of explosive breakthrough. Logic, mathematics and scientific method are such processes, even though our introduction to them may present them as areas of stability immune from change.

But no mind, however original, can be indefinitely receptive. The capacity concept has relevance at the highest imaginative levels as well as at the lowest; this applies with particular force to the originator devoted to working out a chosen line of research. A point will be reached where he is under pressure to resist (treat as noise) whatever is incompatible with his main design, and this may include the contributions of equally gifted workers in his own field. This is a hard fact to reconcile with the scientist's allegiance to objectivity, but it is useless to turn a blind eye to it. In the field of creative endeavour open-mindedness is not enough. The only man who can make any sort of claim to it is the intelligent dilettante, and he can do so only because he has remained uncommitted.

These remarks acquire increasing relevance as the amount and speed of transmission of all kinds of information become more and more intensified. Indeed, the volume of scientific research today and the inability of scientists to keep pace with it has done much to bring about a condition in which fresh concepts are treated like commercial products in an expanding economy. A new theory hits the news, supplies for a while a jargon which is on everybody's lips, then falls away, ousted by something still more recent. This cycle of rise and decline has little to do with the theory's authenticity; it is a manifestation, in an especially inappropriate setting, of a restless search for novelty. If a scientist plays this version of the fashion game, he runs great risk of becoming alienated from his discipline's true course; while an increased accent on research and technology may do much to accelerate the growth of important ideas, the image of a new hypothesis soaring aloft, illuminating the night sky with a short-lived flash, then spending itself like a Guy Fawkes rocket, has little to do with basic scientific advance.

Scientific method, then, is not a static discipline but a process which develops as human consciousness explores its environment. There have, of course, been well-marked stages in this growth and there are occasions when it is justifiable to contrast it with other modes of intellectual activity. Over-sharp definition is a permissible tool of instruction; we cannot, as Wittgenstein hinted, introduce too much relativity into our teaching or the student feels baffled and cheated.

Among the more important phases of methodological growth we may mention deductive reasoning, refined observation, principles of classification and the controlled experiment. Each of these has started life as a branch of philosophy, after which philosophy becomes repudiated as hostile to science. It is, however, wrong-headed to imagine that these early stages have ceased to play an essential role in scientific life. We may have left behind the moment when it was thought that truth could be reached by pure deduction, but that does not mean that we no longer deduce. All that has happened is that the deductive processes have become internalized; men theorize within the precincts of science rather than outside.

From the time of Galileo and Bacon there has been a tendency to equate scientific pursuit with the controlled experiment. Undoubtedly the controlled experiment has been the instrument responsible for most advances in the physical and many of the biological sciences. But if psychology had insisted on a corresponding degree of control in all its studies of human behaviour, it would hardly have got off the ground. If we must insist on a comprehensive definition of all scientific effort, we must limit ourselves to phrases like systematic thinking, trained observation and the scrupulous sifting of evidence. Should it be objected that this admits activities like history and biography, prediction may be added as a fourth heading; we cannot, however, insist on controlled experiment as a *sine qua non* without ruling out most of astronomy and large tracts of geology, botany and zoology.

A similar view must be taken of the 'pure' sciences from which so many of the tools of research have been borrowed. Perhaps borrowed is not the most accurate word; it would be truer to say that there has been interchange between the principles of logic and mathematics and the practical problems of the external world. It would not be difficult to argue that every mathematical branch, from simple arithmetic to decision theory, has come about in response to concrete problems, and it is a useful exercise to try and enter into the intellectual climate that existed before the invention of calculus or probability theory.

35 Psychology and the physical sciences

'The development of physics as "the queen of the sciences" may be regarded as a consequence, in part, of two fundamental conditions: (a) the development of a powerful mathematics built on the axioms of arithmetic, and (b) the fact that these axioms appear to be realized in vast areas of physical phenomena. Consequently, scientists in other areas of knowledge, and in particular social scientists, have not only respected physics but have tried to build their own science in its image. Unfortunately, the second condition above is, in general, not satisfied by social psychological phenomena. It behooves the social scientist to try to formulate axiom systems which satisfy the behaviour he is interested in and to encourage the development of the appropriate mathematics. In its broadest sense, then, this is simply the recommendation that the social scientist attend to his measurement theory.'

Clyde H. Coombs

This quotation from the writing (29) of a well-known measurement theorist describes with fair accuracy the attitude of most psychologists to the achievements of physics. The author makes clear that the limit of application of physical models to the field of psychology is soon reached and urges that the social scientist attend energetically to the development of fresh models reflecting the characteristics of psychological phenomena. He does, however, seem to take for granted that subtlety and precision of measurement afford the final criterion by which every kind of scientific sophistication can be judged. This is surely not axiomatic. It is no doubt true of physics, but to assume that because it is true there it must hold for all other disciplines suggests that the influence of physics is still fostering uncritical assumptions.

The theme of physics is the structure of matter, that of psychology the structure of behaviour. Behaviour is rooted in perception and some of the first findings of experimental psychology (cf. Weber's Law) established the principle that human perception does not reflect the environment in a wholly objective way, but in a way that is influenced by the subject's mental capacity, his prior experience and the context of present perception. In other words, perception is basically an awareness of differences. This relativity theme permeates all human behaviour. It is implicit in problems of human communication in the sense that our reception of information is always affected by that already in our possession. Helson's Adaptation Level, acclaimed by some as one of psychology's major principles, is to some extent a contemporary restatement of the Weber motif extended to cover most of the main areas of behaviour. Whatever may be learned later about the neurological, biochemical and physiological bases of behaviour, it seems unlikely that such knowledge will alter our general conceptions about human response, and an understanding of the principle that underlies this is of far greater account to both theory and practice than the ability to make precise measurement in a restricted field. Without such understanding it is impossible to interpret the implications of measurement, to decide, for example, whether what has been found in the laboratory will hold good in a real-life situation.

Perception and judgement are not passive reflectors of the environment, but operate in a field dictated partly by past experience and partly by the components of the present occasion. Psychology is concerned to investigate mechanisms of this type, and it will be seen that though such investigations call for accurate measurement and an understanding of probability and sampling theory, there is no demand for superfine quantification. Indeed, very fine measurement would often be an irrelevance, as it would be irrelevant to estimate a man's height to a twentieth of an inch.

What has just been said is not, of course, intended to suggest that human actions and judgements must be accepted by the experimenter as units incapable of further analysis. All judgements and actions are the resultants of interacting, conflicting or reinforcing mechanisms, whose nature it is the business of experiment and statistical analysis to identify. But the starting-point of all such inquiries must always be the behaviour of individual subjects whether studied in real life or the laboratory, and behaviour, however controlled or refined, is a gross phenomenon when set against the behaviour of matter in a prepared situation.

What may seem paradoxical is that there is little or no correlation between measurement precision and sophistication of experimental design. Psychological experiments require as much expertise as any other, and it is by virtue of this that psychologists claim that their work is scientific.

The upshot of this argument is that there is a risk that psychology, having torn itself free from philosophy, may immolate itself on the altar of physics. Should this happen, it will be due to a confusion between the aims of measurement and experimentation. There is not a great deal of difference between the methods of various disciplines, but the degree of measurement called for varies enormously from one to another. As a rule the purpose of applying the physical sciences is to forge an instrument or piece of equipment capable of carrying out a narrowly specified task with great accuracy. It would be surprising if such accuracy could be obtained without scrupulous regard for every detail of design. But the salient feature of human behaviour is plasticity rather than precision, and apart from this the concept of design has little meaning in the human context. A man's energies may be directed to the development of skills and the exercise of these may call for a high degree of co-ordination and accuracy; in these settings there is some analogy between man and machine, but in the activities regarded as most specifically human, skills are usually subordinate to more comprehensive ends. The mathematician is more than a calculator, the artist more than a craftsman.

While psychology is concerned with the prediction of behaviour, the goals of prediction are not always self-evident. The implications of this will stand out more clearly when we consider the lines of research appropriate to the three areas of communication. But before we come to this, it is desirable to carry the comparison of the aims of physics and psychology a stage further.

36 The dangers of mechanomorphism

In his chapter 'The influence of language on medicine' *Young* (117) emphasizes both the need for analogies in developing our understanding of the human organism and the effects of unthinking acceptance of the terms used to express them. There is, he points out, a strong tendency to confuse descriptions and facts and to overlook the extent to which 'facts' are dominated by language. Physiologists may smile at Descartes' talk of water-pipes and fountaineers, but many of them have been dazzled by modern imagery, and while the terminology of a Sherrington marks a great advance, 'all our talk of neurons, action potentials and synaptic transmitters has not produced a satisfactory set of methods for dealing with nervous disease'.

What is true of physiology is even truer of psychology, whose long struggle for recognition as a scientific discipline has lent added weight to the fascination of mechanical analogies. The machine as classically conceived enshrines all the attributes of determinism and predictability, and since the ability to predict is the acknowledged hallmark of scientific attainment it is natural that some pulses should quicken when a chance of representing behaviour in mechanical terms offers. What the experimenter's enthusiasm sometimes leads him to overlook is that a mechanical model may simulate behaviour with a high degree of realism and at the same time omit an essential feature. The point may be illustrated somewhat grotesquely by Shannon's well-known orders of approximation to standard English text. Starting with zero-order approximation (symbols independent and equiprobable, e.g. XFOML), he moves through first-order approximation (symbols independent but with frequencies of standard English text, OCRO HLI), second-order (digram structure, ON IE ANTSOUTINYS), third-order (trigram structure, IN NO IST LAT WHEY), first-order word approximation (words chosen independently but with appropriate frequencies, REPRESENTING AND SPEEDILY IS) to second-order word approximation (word-transition probabilities correct but no further structure, THE HEAD AND IN FRONTAL ATTACK ON AN ENGLISH WRITER). At this point we may be wondering if the frontal attack is threatening the English writer by making his job redundant. Reflection suggests that this fear is unnecessary. The orders of approximation have been reached by drawing systematically on the pooled contributions of past writers. Had there been no past writers, there would have been no contributions; hence the writers may be seen as necessary conditions of the approximations. Still, it may be argued, new writers also draw on the pooled contributions of past writers; shall we, then, by applying Shannon's model be able to dispense with writers in the future? The answer to this could be that if a writer does nothing but draw on pooled contributions, there is no reason why he should not be dispensed with; but the writer whose work has survival value will have added as well as drawn.

It is probably unnecessary to add that Shannon's purpose in devising the above model was not to explore the mechanisms of verbal behaviour. What he set out to do was to generate an artificial text which would help him to define and prove theorems relevant to the encoding and transmission of actual English messages through an artificial system.

The appeal of the machine image to the psychologist is offset by the almost universal appeal of the concept of freedom to men and women of all kinds. This concept may be intellectually diffuse and emotionally toned, but millions have died for it and few have succeeded in living without it. This is not the place to analyse the sources of this archetypal notion, but it is necessary to draw attention to its compelling power and the formidable dilemma it poses for psychology. The primacy of the concept is asserted not merely at the level of politics and government but in every field of human activity. Whatever line he is pursuing, whether it be gambling or research, a man cannot rid himself of the notion that however much of his conduct may be predetermined, there is over and above this an element that remains free, that psychologically he is an open rather than a closed system. It may not be possible to demonstrate that this conviction has validity, but it is not difficult to point the distinction between the closed and open aspects of behaviour at the level of an every-day activity. A game such as chess, where every move can be given formal expression and its implications subjected to analysis, lends itself to this kind of demonstration. This pastime, now nearly fifteen hundred years old, has undergone surprisingly little change, and since it became popular in Spain and Italy in the fifteenth century its rules have remained virtually unaltered. During this period full records of innumerable games have been kept and key moves submitted to exhaustive examination. As a result a cumulative lore, a kind of collective memory, has grown up, so that today any player in any country can have access to it and no player can progress far without assimilating its elements. Indeed, a newcomer picking up a standard work on chess openings and noting the endless columns of variations, might carry away the impression that the prime requisite for championship honours was a vast memory store, that the successful player was the one who recalled most frequently the approved move in a given situa-tion. Without belittling the value of analysis or the advantages of strong powers of retention, it can be asserted without hesitation that the appeal of the game cannot be accounted for in this way; more than this, the appeal would fade if a point were reached when the outcome of all possible moves had been evaluated and com-mitted to the individual memory. The fascination of the game lies in the fact that in spite of the huge common denominator of pooled experience, it is still possible for the individual to devise his own strategies and develop a personal style.

What is true of chess holds good of other activities; in fact it would probably be safe to say that all activities that exert a con-tinuing claim on human interest afford the opportunity of developing a cumulative lore without exhausting the possibility of personal manner and expression.

Our two examples, chess and the Shannon language approxi-mations, both illustrate the point that a complex phenomenon can always to a degree be represented in terms of something less complex. A work of literature can be viewed as a sequence of words or letters, a game of chess as a sequence of moves. Such representations transcribe in a systematic and logical way the manifest features by which these processes can be communicated, but they do not transcribe the processes themselves. Similarly, information theory offers a means of transmitting the symbols from which messages can be constructed, and mechanical models of behaviour can transcribe generalized characteristics of the behaviour itself. But all models are derived from past events; language approximations from the past use of words, chess analyses from past games, behaviour models from past performances. On the basis of these poolings it is possible to make certain types of prediction. It is important to know the sorts of prediction that can be made and the sort that cannot. In psychology two kinds are possible. We can say first how people in general are likely to behave in specified conditions, and secondly whether A is more likely to behave in a specified way than B. To say that A is less likely to behave in a specified way than B could mean many things, one of which could be that A is original and creative, so that the details of his performance cannot be anticipated with the same assurance as B's.

While the psychologist as scientific investigator is pledged to extend the principles of measurement and prediction to larger and larger areas of behaviour, he has no grounds for assuming that every aspect of behaviour must prove ultimately measurable. Still less must he ignore the effect that such a belief may have on human beings, for there can be no doubt that we are all influenced in both attitude and performance by the view we take of ourselves and our capacities. The anthropomorphic view may contain elements of vanity and childishness, but at least it presented the human being with a positive self-image; the mechanomorphic view, by underplaying the role of human spontaneity and individual responsibility, could well deject and degrade man in his own eyes, and it would be ironic if the psychologist, to whom many look for guidance, were to reinforce this image through a mistaken notion about scientific integrity.

37 Research on sign communication

In an article referred to earlier *Cherry* (25) examines the analogy between a communication channel and a human operator, and lists some assumptions applying to the former. Communication theory, he points out, is expressed entirely in the language of an external observer, not in that of one of the participants; it is a statistical theory concerning the average, macroscopic properties of a system, not specific momentary properties; the communicants operate with an agreed alphabet of signs, and this alphabet remains unchanged. Against this, the human operator is an integrated organism with interacting sense organs which cannot be compared with independent input terminals; the parameters of his experience are subject to change; he attributes meaningfulness to stimuli, whereas communication theory makes no reference to meaningfulness but merely to syntactic properties and rules, to signs and their probabilities. There are, however, situations where it is possible to ignore meaningfulness, regarding stimuli 'like letters, words, etc., purely syntactically'. When we can do this, 'we are assuming that the responses of a human operator will depend only upon the range of choice they offer and their probability of occurrence'. Where a situation approximates to this condition, it is permissible, in Cherry's view, to apply communication theory to experimental psychology.

While there can be no objection to a communication theorist translating a human situation into his own language, the psychologist must be wary of adopting this language uncritically. He is bound, for example, to ask what is involved in a phrase like 'ignoring meaningfulness', and when he does so he is likely to decide that such situations lend themselves to communication theory not because meaningfulness is irrelevant to the operator but because it is constant for all operators. This is a point of great importance to the main argument of this book and offers an

explanation of why the concepts of information theory have qualitative reference to human communications of every kind. In
the messages transmitted through artificial systems the concept
of meaning does not arise, because the items transmitted are the
symbols from which meaning can be derived, although they possess no meaning in themselves. But all human communication
trades in meaning, the messages which approximate to the
conditions of artificial systems being those where meaning is
fixed, e.g. all motorists on English roads know that a green
traffic light means 'Go' and a red light 'Stop'. If these systems
were replaced by human operators (policemen) their 'Stop' and
'Go' signals might be expected to approach a similar uniformity,
although individual ways of executing arm movements might
introduce a slight degree of ambiguity. If agreement about the
use of arm movements had not been reached, so that one policeman beckoned, a second jerked his head and a third used his voice,
the number of misunderstandings would be greater still. Finally,
if there were no agreement that the function of a policeman was
to tell the motorist when to move and when to wait, communication would be minimal.

The fact that information theory can be applied directly (i.e.
mathematically) to very few human situations is, then, because
very few communications between human beings are wholly
unambiguous. The majority are made up of a core of agreed
meaning fringed with varying shades of peripheral variation.
The factors making for variation have been discussed in Part 2,
one of the chief ones being that the interpretation of most messages is partly dependent on the receiver's state of information.
A second important reason is that human beings operate as open
systems except when they knowingly place themselves within
the context of a closed one. If they did not operate as open
systems, they would be incapable of extending their thoughts
and experiences; to some degree failure in communication is a
penalty that has to be paid for creativeness, which would be
unthinkable if, reverting to the language of communication
theory, men were not free to vary and add to their alphabets.

The practical impetus to the psychologist's study of communication theory has sprung from the need for human beings to
take the role of operators in artificial systems. To do this successfully the operator must narrow his attention to the task of

processing information within the context the system lays down. Many experimental studies have been directed to this end, and those mentioned in the following pages represent only a small cross-section of this effort. Some of the studies have been discussed already; they are mentioned again in the hope of giving continuity to the presentation.

Eighty years ago *Merkel* noted that as the number of choices or alternatives increased, the time taken by the subject to choose from among them increased too. This finding was accepted, but it was left unexplored till *Hick* (51) published a paper on the rate of gain of information, which showed that there was a linear relationship between reaction time and the logarithm of the number of alternatives. This constituted an advance from Merkel's rank-order type of lawfulness to the establishment of a constant rate of gain, which would make it possible to predict the effects of varying the amount of information by extrapolating from existing data. By applying information theory to the field of choice reactions, it thus appeared possible to express the structure of stimulus sequences in statistical terms by the formula

$$\text{Reaction time} = a + bT$$

where a represents a part of the reaction time irrelevant to the process of choice, b is a slope constant and T the amount of information transmitted. It also seemed legitimate to regard $1/b$ as a measure of channel capacity. Subsequent research has suggested that this formula oversimplifies, in that it ignores the relationship between stimulus and response; this, when 'good', is found to give a very low or even a zero value to b. This goodness appears to be the result of practice, the effect of which can be to obliterate reaction-time differences for choices from alphabets of different size. In other words, Hick's finding seems to apply most completely when task learning is at an early stage and to grow progressively less marked as learning proceeds. There are indications that the phenomenon reasserts itself if at any stage the difficulty of the task becomes accentuated, e.g. by being performed under harder conditions. Presumably this is because any such increase of difficulty introduces a new learning element. Thus, if we may throw together the terminologies of psychology and information theory, learning may be regarded as the overcoming of noise, and the rate of gain of information gets flattened as noise is neutralized by practice.

Crossman (31) has explored the noise phenomenon from a different point of view. Noting that the amount of variation in performance under constant conditions is roughly similar for a variety of situations (simple and choice reaction times, absolute judgements expressed on a continuous scale, repeated fast hand-movements to a fixed target), he argues that there may be a general factor at work producing Gaussian variation of 10 per cent to 20 per cent of the mean of any one-dimensional behavioural output not subject to feedback control. By analogy with neuro-physiological work on the mean impulse frequency in single fibres, it seems reasonable to attribute the above findings to in-herent random fluctuations in the central processes. Random varia-tion is recognized as a basic noise factor in artificial systems, and it may be that variations in the brain's nerve impulses produce a corresponding effect on human behaviour.

Weisz and McElroy (109), of the USAF Decision Sciences Labora-tory, have investigated the effects of speed stress on the processing of information in a complex task. If activities varying in type and complexity of information processing are included in a com-plicated task, are there differential effects on performance in the various sub-tasks under increasing levels of speed stress? The task, which consisted basically in identifying specified variations of four geometrical forms (rectangle, trapezoid, triangle and paral-lelogram), included five information processing activities differing in (*a*) spatial and temporal uncertainty of events requiring re-sponse, (*b*) frequency of occurrence of response events, (*c*) short-term memory requirements, and (*d*) perceptual requirements in the recognition of events. Frame times were reduced from 13 sec. through 10 sec., 8 sec., 6 sec. down to 4 sec. High-frequency tasks not requiring search were found to be relatively impervious to stress effects, while lower-frequency events occurring in low-priority display locations gave rise to poorer performance at all stress levels. Significant performance decrement under stress occurred first in the most complex low-probability tasks requiring search and short-term memory. Highly practised subjects were found to have evolved a priority strategy based primarily on the frequency of response events in different display locations. In general, the results were interpreted as similar to findings in the study of vigilance behaviour and statistical decision theory.

Teichner (99) working in the same laboratory, has been concerned with a three-part programme studying the effects of task stress on the processing of information. In Part 1 he studied first the effects of system variables on reporting ability. Here the basic task required the display for one second of slides carrying various amounts of alphabetic data. Six experiments were planned to study the effects of load, delay, presentation rate, response rate, load rate, and display reported on (last seen or last but one). The subjects were highly trained operators in comparable situations. No main effects were found for delays, presentation rates, response rates, or load rates. For slow presentation rates accuracy was poorer when the subject responded to every display rather than only to some. This effect disappeared, however, for the higher presentation rates. The accuracy for the last display seen was greater than for the previous one. It was noted that the subject appeared to reach a limit of performance, which he would not normally attempt to exceed. He also seemed to develop a coding system which permitted him to handle more and more information up to the code's limit, all other information being rejected or filtered out before storage in short-term memory.

In Part 2 Teichner investigated the interaction of short-term and long-term memory through the medium of letter sequences with gaps of varying length. The results showed that the effectiveness of data selection from long-term storage depended upon short-term demands, but failed to demonstrate an interaction of more than nominal interest.

With Part 3 he turned to subjective information as a function of source information. The experiments suggested that subjective information, defined as the amount of information in judgement of the number of different events and frequency of events, was a useful dependent measure for describing stimulus or display events as the subject assesses them. Different phenomena seem to occur when he makes a judgement about a sample from the stimulus or display sources and when he makes judgements from samples about the source itself. Results also suggested that there is an optimum range of redundancy for a given amount of information, that the time rate of presentation is a significant variable and that subjective information first increases and then decreases with an increasing rate.

Turner, Wallace and Wessel (100) (University of Pennsylvania), have examined the effects of excess and redundant information on the speed of information processing, which they define as the 'transformation of a set of input messages into some other set of output messages'. By excess information they mean information that appears useful but is in fact useless, whereas redundancy is the name for substitute information. Both excess and redundant information were found to decrease the speed of task solutions and the number of efficient solutions (those using the smallest number of steps). But only excess material increased the number of mistakes made, although the extent to which this occurred was not great. The studies also noted a small association between mistakes made and the subjects' 'g' levels.

Turner and Wallace in collaboration with *Tear* (98) (also of Pennsylvania) have additionally investigated the effects of previous experience on response in ambiguous situations. Subjects confronted with entirely ambiguous information either did not respond at all or based their responses on past experience.

Glanzer (39) has reported results of a five-year programme (1958–63) under the heading 'Coding and use of information in problem-solving'. He describes his general purpose as studying information processing aspects of problem-solving and other forms of complex phenomena. His study falls into three parts with the titles in 'Problem-solving', 'Encoding perception', and 'Learning and storage of verbal materials'. In the first part he explored seven factors, example sign (positive or negative), concept size, series complexity (amount of superfluous information), information order, storage load, selection load and information rate. He found that the operations fell into two stages, first, the specification and storage of the dimension values, and secondly, the selection of relevant dimensions on the basis of the example information. In a second study of EEG concomitancies he found systematic and predictable changes in alpha rhythm for each solving stage, but marked individual differences for kappa rhythm. This finding conflicts with that of Chapman *et al.*, who found regularity for kappa, but alpha effects weak. Glanzer is now testing the hypothesis that auditory inputs generate clear kappa effects and visual inputs clear alpha effects.

In his encoding experiments, Glanzer started by establishing that the relative difficulty of individual visual stimuli could not be accounted for in terms of information or gestalt theory. From this he formed the hypothesis that his subjects' perceptual processing included a covert verbal encoding and that the length of the verbal code determined the difficulty of each stimulus. He terms this the verbal-loop hypothesis, and claims support for it from experiments using visual black and white stimuli, binary numbers and conventional figures.

Glanzer's third set of experiments examines the hypothesis that serial position effects can be used as a basis for analysing the functions of storage mechanisms in human subjects. Studies in rote-learning situations suggest that these effects cannot be explained in terms of facilitation or inhibition, but only as the result of a strategy adopted by the subject. In free recall situations the subject appears to use both short-term and long-term storage (double-storage hypothesis). This hypothesis finds support in the results of experiments designed to manipulate each type of storage independently.

Wiegand's (113) interest is in the degree to which uncertainty can be considered a fundamental variable underlying the behavioural effects observed in both simple and complex information processing tasks. He claims to show that an area of behaviour traditionally relegated to the limbo of higher mental activities can be subjected to quantification, control and prediction. The situations he has explored include simple reaction times, choice reaction times, and choice reaction times in which complex transformation operations are performed on encoded outputs; in all of these high levels of uncertainty are imposed upon the subject —in the first two the human component acts as a simple transmission channel, in the third as a translation or transformation channel. Wiegand urges that his analytic technique be applied to other higher processes such as decision-making, problem-solving and creative thinking. His general hypothesis is that an organism's reactivity is fundamentally a function of the variety of alternative controlling events with which it is in continual contact. This variety is another name for uncertainty and if this can be controlled so can the organism.

Broadbent has also turned his attention to the uncertainty concept. Noting that the ease with which words are perceived appears to be an effect of their frequency of usage, he has examined in a more general context the interactions between information arriving from the senses and the subject's pre-existing biases. Mathematical models, applied to the prediction of reaction time from a knowledge of the probability with which various stimuli will occur, have been broadly successful. This has led to the identification of noise in a decision system with the amount of uncertainty or incompatibility between each stimulus and its appropriate response. Experiments have been carried out in which each stimulus is tactual stimulation of a finger-tip and each response is pressure of a key by a finger. In some cases the response finger is the one stimulated, in others a different finger. This variable is shown to interact with many others and the results are broadly consistent with the statistical approach.

Weisz, Licklider, Swets and Wilson (110) have produced an interesting theoretical study with the title 'Human pattern recognition procedures as related to military recognition problems'. This discusses clearly, simply and logically the psychological problem of perception in terms of recent mathematical models, particularly that of statistical decision theory. The paper is too long to summarize, but its lucid quality can be conveyed in a couple of quotations:*

1) 'The main trend in the experimental psychology of perception during the last decade has been to analyse perception as a kind of problem-solving. From this approach, one sees the perceiver as an epistemological system, the task of which is to develop and maintain a simple, consistent, informationally economical representation of the world. The perceptual mechanism is continually working not on the problem: "What picture is on my retina? What pattern is in my cochlea?"—but on the problem: "What must I assume about the world in order to make a simple, coherent story of what I know plus what I am now sensing?"'

2) 'In the nervous system, in so far as one can judge from available evidence, there is no clear spatial separation of memory from processing. Both functions may take place in the same tissue, much as they do in the integrators and potentiometers of analogue computers. That arrangement is fundamentally different from the one used in most modern digital computers.

   'In digital computers, the separation of memory from processing is made in part for economic reasons. If the economic factor were not important, it might turn out that memory

* Reprinted by permission of u.s. Office of Naval Research.

units capable of some processing—such as recognizing their names—would be extremely useful. It seems to us, therefore, that attention should be given (a) to ways to overcome the economic obstacle, and (b) to ideas for using components with both mnemonic and processing capabilities.

'Since neuronal networks, of the kind simulated on digital computers by Farley and Clerk, Rochester et al., embody intermixed memory and processing, it may be that advanced theoretical analysis of such networks would clarify the idea. As matters stand, however, it is conspicuous that our best hardware is arranged in a way so different from our best brains. For numerical calculation that may be good. For pattern recognition, it may not be good.'

These quotations highlight two of the ideas that permeate all recent literature on perception and communication. The first is the notion of the brain as an organ whose function is progressive adaptation to the external world. This concept has received bold and comprehensive treatment from *Bremermann* (8) in his paper 'The evolution of intelligence: the nervous system as a model of its environment'.* Of methodology Bremermann writes:

'The methods and standards of critical thought have not changed much since the Greeks . . . The Greeks did not use, however, systematic experiments to check ideas. This is the next step . . . To check a specific idea a specific experience frequently will be useful; thus we see to it that we make such an experience, that is, we make an experiment.

'This is the essence of the experimental part of the scientific method. We improve the human eigen-model by improving the "collection of facts" available to the checking apparatus of the brain in a systematic way.'

and later:

'Our theory agrees with Kant's *Kritik der reinen Vernunft* in emphasizing that our picture of the world depends upon the senses and the structure of the mind. However, while for Kant the structure of the mind is something like a "constant of nature", eternally unchanging, our whole theory is based on the hypothesis that it does change and develop.'

Like Weisz and his co-workers, Bremermann attaches key import-

* Reprinted by permission of U.S. Office of Naval Research.

ance to the 'human recognition apparatus'. 'Experiments of the experimental sciences relate phenomena to this apparatus. Logic usually seemed to be of a quite different nature. But in our theory it appears closely related: in logic, too, we have to rely somewhere on the recognition apparatus, our "intuition", to judge the justifiability of basic axioms and operations.'

The second idea is that of information processing, a phrase that has gained such wide currency that there is danger of failing to ask what else in mental activity remains. Weisz *et al.* make clear that they regard its connotation as limited, i.e. they distinguish processing from memorizing, and their argument suggests that its widespread application stems from recent interest in the digital computer. It is not difficult to discern a parallel between the operations of a digital computer and human intelligence, but there is a risk of being so impressed by the analogy that we may come to assume that all mental operations are reducible to its terms. The view taken in this book is that processing plays a part in all mental activity, but that as the level of this activity rises the processing element recedes in importance. It is at its peak in the performance of learned tasks and the carrying out of routine exercises; in the learning of new tasks and the solving of given problems, the processing role is of considerable but not paramount importance; while in full creative effort this role is reduced yet more. For similar reasons it is impossible to see how the qualitative stages of concept development, for which Piaget has provided so much evidence, can be reducible to processing, though it is not hard to see that development within a given stage may be largely attributable to it. Admittedly these reflections are speculative; much of the work discussed in the present chapter is concerned to throw more light on the processing mechanisms and it is possible that some unexpected findings may come to light. But the wide importance of this issue makes it desirable for it to be studied from more than one point of view, from that of educational psychology as well as communication, from experimental studies of space perception as well as from the angle of decision-making theory.

So much has been said about the virtues of closed systems and attempts at precise measurement that it will be well to end this chapter on a cautionary note. Within their proper context the importance of these matters can hardly be exaggerated, but there is a danger of scientific ways of thinking invading territory where they have no place. The possible outcome of a too controlled language system was envisioned by George Orwell with horrific insight, and it will be salutary to reconsider some of his comments on the aims of Newspeak. It is still some twenty years short of 1984, but already a number of the symptoms he spoke of can be detected in our everyday talk.

The principles of Newspeak*

'. . . In the year 1984 there was not as yet anyone who used Newspeak as his sole means of communication, either in speech or writing. The leading articles of *The Times* were written in it, but this was a *tour de force* which could only be carried out by a specialist. It was expected that Newspeak would have finally superseded Oldspeak (or Standard English, as we should call it) by about the year 2050. Meanwhile it gained ground steadily, all Party members tending to use Newspeak words and grammatical constructions more and more in their everyday speech. The version in use in 1984, and embodied in the Ninth and Tenth Editions of the *Newspeak Dictionary*, was a provisional one, and contained many superfluous words and archaic formations which were due to be suppressed later. It is with the final, perfected version, as embodied in the Eleventh Edition of the *Dictionary*, that we are concerned here.

'The purpose of Newspeak was not only to provide a medium of expression for the world-view and mental habits proper to the devotees of Ingsoc, but to make all other modes of thought impossible. It was intended that when Newspeak had been adopted once and for all and Oldspeak forgotten, a heretical thought— that is, a thought diverging from the principles of Ingsoc—should be literally unthinkable, at least so far as thought is dependent on words. Its vocabulary was so constructed as to give exact and often very subtle expression to every meaning that a Party member could properly wish to express, while excluding all other meanings and also the possibility of arriving at them by indirect methods. This was done partly by the invention of new words, but chiefly by eliminating undesirable words and by stripping such words

* Reprinted from George Orwell's *Nineteen Eighty-four* by permission of Miss Sonia Brownell and Messrs Secker & Warburg.
    Harcourt Brace &World, Inc. Copyright 1949 by Harcourt, Brace & Company, Inc. Reprinted by permission of Brandt & Brandt.

as remained of unorthodox meanings, and so far as possible of all secondary meanings whatever. To give a single example. The word "free" still existed in Newspeak, but it could only be used in such statements as "This dog is free from lice" or "This field is free from weeds". It could not be used in its old sense of "politically free" or "intellectually free", since political and intellectual freedom no longer existed even as concepts, and were therefore of necessity nameless. Quite apart from the suppression of definitely heretical words, reduction of vocabulary was regarded as an end in itself, and no word that could be dispensed with was allowed to survive. Newspeak was designed not to extend but to *diminish* the range of thought, and this purpose was indirectly assisted by cutting the choice of words down to a minimum.'

'The A vocabulary was composed almost entirely of words that we already possess—words like hit, run, dog, tree, sugar, house, field—but in comparison with the present-day English vocabulary their number was extremely small, while their meanings were far more rigidly defined. All ambiguities and shades of meaning had been purged out of them. So far as it could be achieved, a Newspeak word of this class was simply a staccato sound expressing *one* clearly understood concept. It would have been quite impossible to use the A vocabulary for literary purposes or for political or philosophical discussion.'

'Adjectives were formed by adding the suffix -ful to the noun-verb, and adverbs by adding -wise. Thus, for example, speedful meant rapid and speedwise meant quickly.'

'In Newspeak, euphony outweighed every consideration other than exactitude of meaning. Regularity of grammar was always sacrificed to it when it seemed necessary. And rightly so, since what was required, above all for political purposes, was short clipped words of unmistakable meaning which could be uttered rapidly and which roused the minimum of echoes in the speaker's mind.'

'The intention was to make . . . speech as nearly as possible independent of consciousness.'

'Ultimately it was hoped to make articulate speech issue from the larynx without involving the higher brain centres at all.'

Orwell envisaged Newspeak as a lingual Frankenstein designed by tyranny to ensure a uniformly conditioned outlook and to promote standards of approved efficiency, the price of these

attainments being the extinction of affect, of thinking and ultimately of consciousness. That he presented this as the product
of a ruthless totalitarian régime is unfortunate in so far as it
blinds us to subtler forces which in a less blatant way may be
slowly inducing a similar condition. For one thing, *Nineteen
Eighty-four* was written before kid-glove persecution, that is to
say, persecution by smear and send-up rather than by stake and
dungeon, had matured into the sophisticated instrument it is
today. Again, the growing amount of knowledge and information with which the contemporary world is smitten is in itself
a factor favouring over simplified language, as, in a different
way, is the increase in individuals and nations struggling to self-
awareness. No sensible person will object to the spread of knowledge or education, but it is not sensible to turn a blind eye to
their side-effects. Inventors of language systems such as Basic
English (which must have been known to Orwell) are usually
careful to point out that they are not offering a substitute for the
native tongue, but it does not follow that circumstances will
always respect their intentions. Some of the Newspeak details,
foreseen more than twenty years ago, have already established
themselves in today's English, and it would be complacent to
accept all such innovations as natural and vital evolution. Some
are far from vital and the reverse of natural.

38 Research in the communication of cognitive content

THIS chapter presents a daunting challenge. So much has been written about the relation of sign and meaning, inquiries into linguistic behaviour have been pursued from such a variety of standpoints, that it is difficult to decide on the best point of entry. In the belief that the directest approach is often the most suitable, I will start by reiterating my initial argument about the study of human communication and then lay down the sense in which the key terms are to be understood. Once again, then, studies in this field made no progress till it had become possible to invent artificial systems and to devise a mathematical technique to measure their essential properties. Artificial systems depend upon alphabets of signs that are incapable of acquiring meaning, whereas in human systems there is an irresistible tendency for signs to acquire meaning and for meanings to change and develop. One of the evidences of this tendency lies in the difficulty of finding a term that conveys denotation without connotation. All the words that spring to mind to link token with object—sign, mark, symbol—turn out to be double-edged. Each has been applied in innumerable situations to convey the notion of a purely conventional association, but in every case usage has resulted in an accretion of ideas and images, so that signs, marks and symbols all end by doing something more than indicate.

In view of what has just been said, it may seem perverse to select the word sign for use in an artificial context, to set 'sign' against 'meaning', when, in the discussion of linguistic problems, it has been customary to talk of signs acquiring meaning. The answer to this must be that our understanding of man-made systems compels us to remould our thinking about communication in general. We now have to face for the first time the phenomenon of signs that do not acquire meaning, for which the concept of meaning has no meaning. To make the implications of this quite clear, it may help to postulate five stages of information:

1) The information transmitted in man-made systems consists of symbols drawn from defined alphabets with the properties of closed systems. It is not possible to alter or add to these alphabets once they have been adopted.

2) The human being can (a) assume a role within the context of a man-made system, (b) enter into a few situations (mostly laboratory experiments) which approximate to the conditions of an artificial system. His success in doing this is dependent on the messages he receives and transmits having virtually a fixed meaning. It is impossible to define meaning without some reference to consciousness. Thus symbols transmitted artificially have no meaning for the system which transmits them, but the same symbols transmitted by a human operator have a meaning—though a predetermined one—for him.

3) In other situations the human being behaves at least partly as an open system, which means that the messages he communicates contain potential ambiguity. The majority of cognitive messages thus contain an element of agreed meaning and an element of the subjective. But this ratio of agreed and subjective is not a fixed one. Even if we assume that the meaning of a message is completely clear to the sender (which is by no means always the case), the degree of subjectivity varies from one receiver to another, being dependent on the individual receiver's perception and state of information.

4) In addition, messages can carry affective overtones and the perception of these can vary even when the cognitive content is fully received. In this respect affective content may be regarded as an overlaid function, rather as, in a vastly wider context, speech is an overlaid function of breathing.

5) Finally, intellectual systems (logical, mathematical, technological) arise with implicit agreement about fundamental axioms. These systems operate as large-scale closed systems, but it is important to remember that none of these possess finality; sooner or later saturation is reached and it then becomes necessary to discard or enlarge the system so as to incorporate fresh data from the external world. These enlargements cannot be made in terms of the closed system itself; to make them it is necessary to break the closure and revert to 'open' thinking.

The third of the above stages supplies the theme of the present chapter. Let us start by considering how the meaning of a given word can change. *Webster* (108) traces the history of the word psyche over three hundred years of early Greek history. In Homer psyche means breath of life, a breath believed to reside all over the body and to be forced out of the body (through wound or mouth) in death. It survived after death and was apt to reappear as a man's shadowy replica. With the lyric poets a century later the meaning shifts from breath to seat of emotion, and with the first philosophers successively from source of motion to organ of conscious control (Anaximenes), immortal person (Pythagoras), and thinking soul (Heracleitus). This transition reflects, in Webster's view, the change-over from a primitive to a modern way of reflection, in which awareness of cause and functional relation plays a much greater part. In terms of verbal meaning there is a tendency to shift from physical concept (breath) via process (moving) to hypostatized abstract (soul), and in terms of syntax from simple sentences of equal value to periodic sentences with a free structure of subtly connected clauses. Transitions of this sort are held to constitute a spontaneous device for communicating and developing a gradual change of outlook. They are not, of course, peculiar to the Greeks, although so complete a movement of thought had been experienced by comparatively few peoples before modern times.

Charles Morris (79), philosopher and behaviourist, has done as much as any living writer to analyse and define semiotics (the science of signs) and in doing so to resolve the global concept of meaning into related areas. He distinguishes three main elements in the sign process, namely sign, interpreter and signification. The essence of the sign is a capacity to induce a disposition in the interpreter which will lead him to bring about a certain state of affairs; it is this state of affairs to which the term signification is applied. Syntactics is the study which inquires into the way signs are combined; semantics explores the relationships between signs and significations. Both these studies are highly relevant to communication, although syntactic and semantic are not, of course, psychological terms.

Miller's Language and Communication (76) is still the best review by a psychologist of the psycho-linguistic theme. Begun in 1946 as an attempt to provide graduate courses with a text on the psychology of communication, it matured in book form five years later. Written from a mildly behaviourist viewpoint, it conveys in clear and graceful prose a considerable range of experimental fact and statistical data. The chapters on the phonetic approach and the perception of speech are particularly well done. Sections of special interest bear the titles 'Vocalization of information', 'Relative frequency of phonemes', 'Statistical indicators of style', 'The estimation of readability', 'The organization of verbal behaviour', 'Effects of verbal habits on perception' and 'Communication nets'. The following highly digested statements may, it is hoped, give some idea of the scope of the experimental work recounted in this valuable book:

1) *Speech characteristics of two students* (Sanford). Eleven samples of speech or writing from each subject were scored for more than 200 variables (number of cognitive verbs used, number of subordinate clauses, length of sentences, repetitiveness, etc. etc.). The subjects were compared in respect of each variable, the comparisons after appropriate statistical treatment yielding a rounded picture of each man's style. The study is limited to a comparison of two individuals and a similar analysis of the habits of a larger (control) sample would admittedly enrich the picture.

2) *Restricted telephone nets* (Heise and Miller). Five patterns of three-member telephonic channels were set up, the subjects being in different rooms. Each had his own microphone and earphones over which he could speak and hear messages. If a talker was connected to two listeners (see diagram),* he always

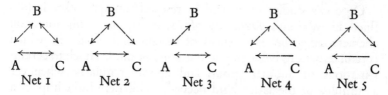

talked simultaneously to both of them. A known amount of white noise was introduced from time to time; this masked the speech and produced errors that had to be corrected before the group could continue. A variety of problems were set with the broad objective of finding which net was most noise resistant and so best at transmitting a clear picture of the group's pattern of information. Comparison for three types of problem

* Reprinted from G. A. Miller's *Language and Communication* (1963) by permission of McGraw–Hill Publishing Company Ltd.

showed that the group's goal must be specified before it is possible to predict the effect of controlling the channels in the net. An optimal arrangement for reaching one goal may not remain optimal when the goal is changed.

3) *Linguistic change* 'A method for studying analogic change consists in teaching an artificial language to a group of subjects, then carefully studying the analogic tendencies that develop. It has been shown with artificial languages that the changes that occur frequently while the subject is first learning the language are the same changes that recur after the language is well learned. If this applies to English, it would mean that the child who, in first learning the words, frequently confuses "uncle" and "aunt" is the one who later will be most apt to show this confusion and interference by a mixture of the two.' An outline of an experiment by *Wolfle* follows in illustration.

Information theory measures information in terms of uncertainty reduction, but this is unrelated to information as content. Does it make sense to talk about measuring content, and if it does, how are we to set about it? In 'The nature and measurement of meaning' (82) *Osgood* dismisses existing approaches (physiological, learning, perception, association and scaling methods), as inadequate, and goes on to develop a semantic differential which he puts forward as a general method of measuring meaning. This technique has since been elaborated in a book *The Measurement of Meaning* (83) and has attracted widespread interest.

Osgood's studies originated in research on synaesthaesia (defined in Warren's *Dictionary of Psychology* as 'a phenomenon characterizing the experiences of certain individuals, in which certain sensations belonging to one sense or mode attach to certain sensations of another group and appear regularly whenever a stimulus of the latter kind occurs'). This definition implies a sort of 'neural short-circuiting' present in only a few individuals, but later investigation showed that such phenomena were by no means rare, e.g. 13 per cent of Dartmouth College students were found to indulge in colour-music synaesthesia. (It is probable that artists have always taken these phenomena for granted. Thus a recent broadcast on Sibelius remarked, 'To him there was always a mystical union between sound and colour.' In 1927 the music critic W. J. Turner discussed the 'colour' of different composers, and about the same time Edith Sitwell was exploiting synaesthaesia in poetry: 'And night came sounding like the growth of trees'.)

Karwoski, Odbert and Osgood decided to explore the mechanisms of inter-modal translation by asking photistic visualizers to 'draw' a simple clarinet tone that grew louder and then softer. Formal analogies could be detected in the various devices employed, one subject representing loudness by thickening of line, another by stronger saturation of colour, a third by increased amplitude of vibration. In a second experiment subjects who had never thought of seeing things when they heard music were instructed to 'force themselves to draw something to represent what they heard'. They produced much the same types of visual forms as the experienced visualizer. From these and other studies Osgood decided that the imagery found in synaesthaesia was on a continuum with metaphor and that both expressed semantic relations.

The next question was whether these relations were dependent upon culture or whether they reflected more fundamental determinants common to the human species. A study of anthropological field reports on five widely separated primitive cultures showed that the generality of some of the relationships was quite striking (e.g. good things were regularly represented as 'up' and 'light', bad things as 'down' and 'dark').

Stagner and Osgood went on to develop a series of seven-step scales (kind–cruel, rough–smooth) on each of which their subjects were asked to place given concepts (Where on each scale would you place 'eager', 'burning'?). They produced fifty of these scales and asked 100 subjects (college students) to judge a number of concepts in terms of each, i.e. with twenty concepts each student was required to carry out a 1,000-item test. The resultant matrices were factor analysed yielding an 'evaluative' factor which accounted for by far the largest portion of the variance, a 'strength' factor, an 'activity' factor, and several that could not be identified in the first approximations.

The semantic differential has undergone considerable evolution over the past dozen years. Its central ideas are first identification of the main factors entering into semantic description and judgement, secondly the selection of specific scales corresponding to these factors and their use as a standardized measure of meaning. This differential makes it possible to specify quantitatively the meaning of a particular concept to a particular individual. The theoretical relevance of this to the problem of communication between two individuals will be clear; given any message, the differential could go some way towards helping us decide to what degree the message is open to subjective distortion. It is hardly possible to employ the instrument as specifically as this in a real-life situation, and it seems likely that its chief practical value will lie in group rather than individual contexts. To establish variations in the meaning attributed to common concepts by different cultures, age-groups and sexes should have considerable import for social and educational psychology. This point is borne out by the contents of a symposium on the semantic differential held at a recent congress of the British Psychological Society. Papers were presented in which judgements and assessments were compared for Conservatives, Socialists and Liberals (Gardiner) (37), adolescent boys and adolescent girls (Hallworth and Waite), obsessive patients, psychopathic patients and control in-patients (Marks). The technique was further discussed as a scientific instrument seen from the psycho-physical standpoint (Meredith), from the angles of reliability and validity (Warr and Knapper), and on mechanical models implicit in the concepts of semantic differential data (White). As its name implies, the differential touches only semantic sources of distortion; syntactical sources are a separate issue amenable to different techniques.

R. S. Lilly (67) has carried out a valuable developmental study of the semantic differential, the purpose of which was to consider the primary dimensions of affective meaning for children at four age levels. Earlier attempts to investigate this area had suggested that children's processes were based on fewer dimensions than those of adults, but the present study finds little difference between them; for example, a high degree of consistency in regard to Osgood's three primary dimensions, evaluation, potency and activity, appears at each age.

Lilly's work is additionally significant for the employment of three-mode factor analysis, a recent technique that was not available to Osgood in his early studies. There are three sources of variance in an SD study, concepts, scales and subjects. Previous inquiries have been restricted to the dimensions of the scale mode, i.e. of the bipolar adjective scales (good–bad, hard–soft) in terms of which each concept had to be judged. The present investigation makes it possible to identify the factors underlying concepts also; thus a first factor, interpreted as human, loads heavily on concepts like My Mother, Me, Doctor and Policeman, while the first scale factor (evaluation) weighs powerfully in pairs such as good–bad and kind–cruel. The third mode of analysis makes it possible—theoretically at least—to divide respondents into a number of types each with its own loading pattern in respect of the other modes; in other words, it throws light on the cognitive and affective patterns that differentiate one human being from another.

Schroder and Blackman (91) (Princeton University) have recently examined the possible contributions of multi-dimensional scaling techniques to a closely related goal, the measurement of conceptual dimensions. Their theoretical point of departure may be given in their own words:

> 'Attitudes, needs and other aspects of personality may be viewed as information processing structures. For example, an attitude is seen as a structure which selects units of information about stimuli in the outside world and combines or organizes this information for memory storage and action. In this model, any information processing structure consists of:
> a) A number of dimensions along each of which information can be arranged in a single rank order.
> b) Combinatory rules which organize a number of dimensions of information.'

The MDS model assumes that in making judgements people may combine one, two or more attributes of objects. In ordinary psychological scaling, persons judge one attribute at a time, this attribute having been named by the experimenter. In MDS the bases or attributes to be used are not given. Instead subjects are required to make some global judgement (How alike are USA and USSR? USA and UK? etc.) and MDS is then used to discover the attributes underlying such judgements and the rules governing their combination. What part, for example, does the capitalist–communist antithesis play in the formation of such judgements compared with the dimension military strength–military weakness? The authors conclude that 'combinations in which selective or complex organizational rules are employed cannot as yet be identified by multi-dimensional scaling. However, research in social psychology and personality demonstrates that salience and

o

other selective rules are often used. Progress in the objective measurement of such combinatory rules will make an enormous contribution to psychology.'

Skemp (93), conscious of the difficulties of applying current learning theories to problems of teaching, has devoted much effort to the production of a schematic learning theory intended to make good this defect. Theoretically he seeks to link the schema concept (as understood by Bartlett and Hebb) with Piaget's processes of assimilation and accommodation. Experimentally the aim has been to test the teaching value of artificial schemas based on symbols with associated meanings that can be compounded to express more and more complex themes. Thus single visual symbols may be used to indicate writing, information, movement and electricity, the four symbols together standing for a telegram. The main purpose of these experiments is to demonstrate the superiority of schematic over rote learning, but by schematic Skemp means something more than meaningful. The latter word has been commonly applied to subject matter invested with interest; e.g. learning the names of bones and muscles would be thought of as rote learning, compared to which demonstration of their place and function on a living body would be meaningful. But schemas are chosen to carry meaning themselves and to facilitate the growth of meaning through easy combination. The word schema will bring to mind the barrier referred to earlier as incompatibility and it will be found valuable to relate the two contexts. It seems probable (*a*) that people taught the same subject through different schematic approaches will find it hard to establish common ground for discussion, (*b*) that bad as well as good learning schemas can be devised, and that one of the effects of a bad schema will be difficulty in building up a coherent store of information.

Studies of the language barrier have been made by *Black* (7) (Ohio State University), who has experimented on loss of intelligibility arising from morphemes (vocabulary), syntax and phonemes (pronunciation). Typical results show native American students with normal hearing achieving 80 per cent success when listening through a 1-db signal-to-noise ratio, American students with mild hearing loss achieving comparable success with a 3-db ratio, and foreign students advanced in the study of English reaching the same level with a 6-db ratio. Black has also experimented with four methods of speech deterioration: reduced intensity, variation of signal-to-noise ratio, interruption, and the obliteration of segments of weak intensity. After determining the effect of each of the four methods, at six different levels, he investigated the hypothesis that the simultaneous effect of any two of the deterrents would be the joint probability of the two single effects. The hypothesis appeared to be well founded.

Goldman Eisler (41) has examined the relation between speech hesitation and information given by the speaker. Her subjects were shown cartoons from the *New Yorker* with instructions to look at each till its point had been seen, to describe the content of the cartoon story and to formulate its meaning or moral. The process was repeated six times, so that in all there were seven editions of each description and summary, ranging from planned preconceived speech action to routine automatic action. The main findings were first that pause length per word was considerably longer in the summaries than in the descriptions, pause length being inversely related to redundancy; secondly, the length of pauses within sentences was found to be a function of the predictability of the words that followed them; thirdly, comparison of initial delays and within-sentence hesitations makes clear that at least two factors are responsible for hesitation in speech. One is the predictability of words in context which is closely related to the amount of freedom to choose among words at different points of continuous speech; the other is the economy of recoding information, which is greatest before the beginning of a new sentence and increases with the level of abstraction and the scope of generalization.

39 Research in the communication of affective experience

AFFECTIVE experience presents the investigator with a slippery surface, and it is not surprising to find that studies in its communication have been comparatively infrequent. Where they have been attempted, the accent has tended to be on individual differences. This may seem surprising, seeing that such studies usually stem from a search for general principles. Thus the basic question behind Osgood's work on the differential was 'Is it possible to measure cognitive meaning?' not 'How much does A differ from B in his capacity to receive cognitive messages?' It would appear unnatural to set about the second without securing a foothold in the first. It is highly unlikely that the group of psychologists whose work we are about to discuss would unwittingly have put the cart before the horse, and it seems certain that the approach they have chosen was dictated by the extraordinary difficulty of framing an experimental situation which offered any hope for this type of measurement. The reasons for this difficulty are complicated; one of the more obvious ones is that whereas it is possible to frame messages free of affective content, it is not possible to produce communications untouched by cognition. In general cognitive messages are carriers of affect; there are no purely affective messages.

The studies reported by Davitz in his book *The Communication of Emotional Meaning* (34) mark a bold and original venture into largely uncharted land. He and his co-workers start from the point that the existence of non-verbal, emotional communication has been established (there is reference to Darwin's 'expression of the emotions in men and animals'), but that no systematic attempt has been made to follow this up. Their book claims with some justification to constitute such an attempt, but Davitz is concerned to point out that all the studies relate to the communication of *assumed* emotion; the underlying affective states of the subjects

212

are not considered, merely the success or failure of different senders in projecting emotions and the success of receivers in identifying the emotions intended. There is an obvious parallel with the actor-audience situation; there is no simple way of telling how far the actor experiences the states he projects, or how far members of the audience enter into the emotions projected. But undoubtedly some actors project more successfully than others, while some spectators are quicker and more accurate than others in identifying projected moods and emotions.

One experimenter (*Beldoch*) (6) is interested in cross validation between sensitivity to emotional expression in three modes, verbal, musical and pictorial. The verbal material consisted of a paragraph of neutral meaning spoken by a variety of senders to convey specified emotions. In the musical study the same technique was used, set phrases doing duty for the paragraph, while in the pictorial study abstract patterns, created by artists to communicate the same affective repertory, were screened for the subjects to identify. For each of the three presentations reliability coefficients between ·60 and ·70 were found. Comparisons of the subject's scores for the different presentations showed significant correlations for each pair of sensitivities, suggesting a general sensitivity factor. Vocabulary test scores correlated with the ability in each mode, but two of the inter-modal correlations were shown to be independent of the V-element. Background training and art interest did not associate significantly with the sensitivity measure.

In discussing the relation between vocabulary and emotional sensitivity, Beldoch refers to Langer's distinction between discursive and non-discursive symbols. In Langer's view, word meanings are dependent on discursive symbols which are held to be verifiable, duplicable and to have a defined syntax and order, whereas non-discursive symbols depend on personal perception, intuition and direct insight. On the basis of this distinction she interprets art as communication in the non-discursive mode. Beldoch argues that his study suggests a positive relationship between discursive (vocabulary) and non-discursive (vocal, musical and pictorial) symbols, but with considerable independent variance. 'If emotional sensitivity, therefore, can legitimately be accounted for in terms of non-discursive symbolizations, the task of research is to discover the psychological principles of this kind of ability, just as Spearman, Thurstone and others have discovered the principles of discursive intelligence.' In this argument we are wholly with Beldoch. Langer appears to be attributing total objectivity to discursive symbols and total subjectivity to non-discursive. If this sharp distinction were valid, we should expect to find well-nigh perfect communication when messages are dependent on word meaning and total absence of agreement with non-discursive messages. But this is not what we do find.

In another study Levy (65) finds positive relationship between the ability to express feelings vocally and the ability to identify feelings expressed vocally by others; similarly, between either of these and the ability to identify one's own vocal expressions. She further established a relation between verbal intelligence and each of these three abilities, but found the original significances sustained when the effects of intelligence were controlled.

Perhaps the most important chapter comes from Davitz himself in exploring the relation between emotional sensitivity and (a) personality variables, (b) perception and cognition. Using four well-known measures of personality (Guilford–Zimmerman, Allport-Vernon-Lindzey, Edwards, MMPI), he discovered no association between any of thirty-three personality variables and the ability to identify vocal expressions of emotion, whereas all four cognitive measures (Seashore's auditory discrimination, Raven's 1947 matrices, knowledge of vocal characteristics, verbal intelligence) were found to be positively related, the four variables in combination yielding a multiple r of ·60 with the sensitivity measure. This strongly suggests that, at least within the context of the present studies, communication of emotional meaning is a function of cognition rather than of personality.

Other chapters study the ability to identify emotional meaning at successive age levels from 5 to 12 years (Dimitrovsky), the relation between vocal and facial media of expression (Levitt), sensory compensation and judgements of affect by the blind (Blau), and schizophrenics as judges of vocal expressions of emotional meaning (Turner).

Finally, Davitz evaluated four auditory vocal cues (loudness, pitch, timbre, rate) in respect of Osgood's valence, strength and activity considered as variables of emotional meaning. He found a statistically significant correlation for activity with each cue, but nothing significant for strength and valence. He concludes from this that the latter are communicated by subtler or more complex cues.

The upshot of these studies is that the communication of emotional meaning appears to be made possible by a type of perception independent of verbal meaning. Individuals are endowed with it in varying degrees, and there is a suggestion that it matures spontaneously rather as general intelligence is believed to. This is probably in line with ordinary observation, as with the findings of most of the isolated studies of communication by gesture, voice and facial expression which Davitz set out to consolidate. It is encouraging to find further investigations starting up, e.g. McGee (72) (Dartmouth College) is conducting research on non-verbal speech factors on behalf of the American Army. His starting-point is that there are two aspects of speech communication determining the total effectiveness of message transmission. The one that has received the preponderance of research effort is verbal content or word intelligibility. McGee's attention is directed to the other aspect encompassing voice quality, inflectional patterns and other factors that make up voice affect. We should again remind ourselves that Davitz' work has been limited to the study of assumed emotion. There is still nothing but personal observation and experience to guide us in regard to the transmission of spontaneous affect. It is possible that studies such as McGee's may take us further in this direction.

Having postulated emotional perception as a form of mental activity in its own right, we should go on to say a word on the difficult issue of extra-sensory perception—difficult because, although it is more than fifty years since McDougall examined the activities of the Psychical Research Society and more than thirty since *Rhine* pioneered his researches, there is still no agreement among psychologists about the authenticity of paranormal phenomena. A short statement by a Russian biologist (*M. Kantorovich*) (59) on 'Thoughts at a distance' presents the matter in a cool and positive way. Telepathy, according to Kantorovich, is possible but its mechanism is unknown. In support of the first assertion, he cites the evidence of male night moths, marked with paint and transported to a distance six to eight kilometres from the female moth. Some of these males succeed in rejoining the female within forty minutes, even when the female's call has been propagated against the wind. In discussing possible explanations, Kantorovich asserts the existence of real radio connections in the animal world and suggests that biological radio connection probably accounts for this phenomenon. He is in no doubt that living organisms possess many unrevealed possibilities for obtaining information from the outside world, a thought that no student of human communication can afford to ignore.

In orienting ourselves towards lines of future research, it may help to compare the three types of perception in respect of two important attributes, generality and consistency. Cognitive perception, as ordinarily understood, is a basic activity practised by all human beings. We would obviously admit that perceptions become qualified by experience and that individual perceptions will differ as a result of this and of variations in mental endowment, but we should assume that men share the same basic perceptions, since these are rooted in experiences common to us all. We might be prepared to grant that our ideas about a tree or a car might vary more than the use of these common words suggests, but we should be astonished to meet someone who professed to have no perception of cars or trees at all.

With emotional perception our assumptions are much less general. We talk of those who are highly sensitive to expressions of feeling and of those who are conspicuously lacking in this respect. The terms negative and positive psychic are sometimes used as labels for these extremes. It is true that the more sophisticated may ask if this opposition is as great as it appears, whether the grossly insensitive repress evidence rather than fail to assimilate it, and that we do not know the complete answer to such a hypothesis. The work of Davitz, Beldoch, etc., implies that emotional sensitivity is distributed along a continuum, that A is in general more sensitive than B, and B than C; their view, in short, is a refinement of everyday assumptions. There is, however, nothing that points to inconsistency in the perceptions of an individual; a man is not found to be on form one day and wholly deficient the next.

There is evidence neither of generality nor of consistency when we turn to extra-sensory perception. Although those alleged to possess ESP sometimes speak of it as an activity latent in everyone, no evidence has been put forward to suggest that more than a very small minority in fact evince it. Thus the results of the great majority of Rhine's subjects fall well within expectation. Further, there is nothing like consistency even for the small number of positive subjects. The most successful do not score 25 out of 25, as would be expected in any study of day-to-day perception; what Rhine claims are regular 11s to 15s as compared with chance expectations in the region of 3 to 7. Whatever future research may lay bare, it is beyond doubt that today the theme of paranormal psychology is emotionally overheated, suspended uneasily between extremes of credulity and scepticism. The credulity presents no problem, loose and wishful thinking being a universal phenomenon. But scepticism, which starts as a rational refusal to entertain unsupported evidence, is sometimes carried to a point of non-acceptance which becomes in turn irrational. The sources of this irrationality constitute a topic for psychological research as valid as any other.

40 Summary and conclusions

EVERY communication involves three terms, a sender, a message and a receiver. In studying it we can conceive it as a bond between sender and receiver, a kind of manifestation of the subject–object relationship; or we can direct our attention to the main attributes of messages and work our way back from these to the psychology of the participants. The first approach exerts a certain appeal in that it underlines the importance of the theme, presenting it as a symbol of human and social achievement. We can, if we choose, regard the communicative act as a special instance of the organism in relation with its environment, or we can reverse the order and see perception, the basic link between man and his external world, as the prototype of communication. It is a good thing to be alive to these considerations which should discourage us from viewing our theme too narrowly, but the value of such an approach, as of many other broad conceptions, is inspirational rather than practical.

It is the second approach that has dictated the plan of this book. We began by considering the qualities of a particular type of message, went on to admit two further types, and have been concerned since in looking at these from the angle of the main barriers to reception, from that of their relative prominence in a variety of human activities, and from that of the range of problems they set psychological research.

The first chapters examined the link between the type of information transmitted in man-made systems and the information that passes from one human being to another. The motive for doing this lay in the infiltration of information-theory concepts into psychology and a wish to see how far this model can be pressed in the service of research. This type of information has been referred to as sign information, a sign being defined as an element in a closed system, i.e. one with a finite alphabet consisting of units whose probability of occurrence is known. In this sense a sign is a conventional mark, without undertones, associations or nuances, which cannot serve the interests of a sender's personal expression.

To the question 'Does sign information possess meaning?' the answer is that the concept of meaning is inseparable from that of consciousness. Thus within the context of a wholly automatic system signs have no meaning, but place a human operator within such a system and it does violence to language to assert that they have no meaning for him. What is important is that their meaning is fixed and cannot be varied. In the human context, content and sign information must be differentiated not in terms of presence and absence of meaning but in terms of its variability or fixity. The principles of information theory can be applied to human communication up to the point that sender and receiver interpret the words they use identically; it is, however, almost impossible in practice to know how far such agreement exists. Language, even as used by highly educated people, masks all sorts of variability that never comes to the surface. Thus the human situations in which there is any hope of using information theory as a measurement technique will be few and somewhat artificial. On the other hand, all communication is dependent on some degree of agreement, and it is by virtue of this that the concepts of information theory can be enlightening even when the theory cannot be applied in a quantitative way.

Language, the main vehicle of content information, was evolved in response to particular objects and occasions. Information so derived results from a transaction between subject and object; hence it will always contain a subjective element, however small. What A and B mean by book will be close enough for most practical purposes, but there will be the odd occasion when A's interpretation differs from B's. The same cannot be said of their use of sign information, which is dependent on the acceptance of a defined code. Thus words, sentences, etc., possess a peripheral variation which signs do not. Many factors contribute to this variation, including the individual's interests, his past experience, his level of understanding, his sensory acuities and the selectivity of his responses. While the variability can be greatly exaggerated by undisciplined observation and thinking, as well as by intrusions of affect, it is mistaken to think that it can ever be completely eliminated. In the last analysis it is a function of fantasy and intuition which are prerequisites of creative thinking. It is true that logical, mathematical and scientific thinking seem to aspire to the condition of closed systems, seeking to define their terms so as to exclude peripheral variation. But this is really a provisional condition, even though it may be sustained for a very long time (cf. the life span of Aristotelean logic and Euclidean geometry); eventually the limits of application are met, and when this happens advance cannot come from the resources of the system alone. The investigator is forced back into the untidy world of direct experience before he can extend his grasp any further. Osgood's semantic differential is an attempt to identify the common core of meaning in language. The amount of variance left unaccounted for by his factorial technique may be taken as a very rough index of the part played by peripheral variation in the understanding of general terms.

Failures in the communication of sign messages in artificial systems are due mainly to the limited capacity of the receiver or to the injection of unwanted noise. These failures have their counterparts in human communication, but here there are additional sources of breakdown. The chief of these have been termed unstated assumption, incompatibility of schemas, and the intrusion of unconscious and partly conscious mechanisms. Over and above these we have spoken of confused presentation as a generic term for a miscellany of visual, semantic and syntactic factors whose characteristic is to retard understanding rather than promote misunderstanding. Finally there are innumerable failures which cannot be laid to the door of sender, message or receiver, but to the lack of facilities to bring the appropriate parties into contact.

In looking at current research programmes into the transmission of sign and content information, it was found (as might have been expected) that the first is largely concerned with identifying the mechanisms of processing, the second in exploring the semantic and syntactic aspects of content and measuring their effects. Studies of the first kind make free use of information-theory concepts, viewing the central nervous system as a channel with limited capacity, which is in constant danger of being overloaded by unregulated input. This line of work is still of great importance both theoretically and practically; in the beginning it supplied the stimulus to nearly all the work on human communication and its influence remains. It is perfectly natural that, the foundations having been laid on the soil of comparatively simple activities, the practitioners in this field should turn their attention to higher activity levels. At the same time there is sometimes a tendency to speak as though all mental activity can be resolved into processing terms. While it may be hard to say just where processing stops, there seems no justification for such a sweeping assumption. It is not disputed that processing plays some role in every kind of activity, but its importance appears to diminish as activity grows more complex. Research may lead to a modification of this view, but it has provided no evidence in that direction so far.

In trying to assess the trends of this first research line, three broad themes of especial interest appear. The first concerns the interplay of short-term and long-term memory. The extreme contrast between the evanescence of the former and the near permanence of the latter sometimes obscures the fact that the growth and development of the second is dependent on material supplied by the first.* It is more than thirty years since Bartlett's anatomy of remembering drew attention to the many ways the individual can operate on fresh input, and reintroduced the concept of schema as a link between new and past experience. The relevance of this to the reception of information will be obvious, as will the importance of solving outstanding problems in this area.

Secondly, the application of the binary digit as a measure of sign information has underlined the value of a reliable unit of quantity in communication studies. The bit is not a psychological unit and its application is only meaningful in situations where approximation to that of an artificial system is possible. We quoted Broadbent's card-sorting example, where it was possible to apply the unit to one element but not to the second which depended on qualitative variation in stimulus properties. At the same time, no one would dispute that it is easier to discriminate bright red than dark red from black, and a comparative judgement

---

* Reynolds and Rosenblatt point out in their recent annotated bibliography of short-term memory (90) that there is still debate as to whether short-term and long-term memory follow the same laws and undergo the same processes. One interpretation holds that they are both continuous processes, explained by associative learning theory; the other (the view favoured here) that STM is subject to rapid trace decay.

is a first step towards quantification. A unit of psychological effort in terms of which the ease or difficulty of tasks could be measured would be a welcome addition to the research worker's armoury, but no one is likely to underrate the complications inherent in providing one.

Thirdly, the transfer of ways of thinking from the situation they were designed to solve to analogous areas is to be recommended as a fertilizing agency, but demands careful surveillance from those who effect the transfer. It is essential to mark the point where fact gives place to metaphor and it is sometimes easy to overlook this. When it is stated that an alphabet of sixty-four symbols has been chosen for a certain purpose, the statement falls squarely in the realm of fact; the requirements of the proposed system have been weighed and a decision taken as to what will meet the case. Once we are familiar with this line of reasoning there may be a temptation to apply it analogically elsewhere. This is where danger can creep in. We may note, for example, that English speech is built on forty or so phonemes drawn from a possible repertory of several hundred; we must, however, resist the suggestion that the forty phonemes were chosen because it had been decided that this was the smallest number from which speech could be woven to express whatever Englishmen might want to express. It is possible that the use of a relatively small 'alphabet' of phonemes was loosely related to functional requirement, but that is the limit of what can be imputed.

The affective type of message is harder to get to grips with, since, so far as communication goes, affect appears as an overlaid function of cognition. Thus a message designed to convey nothing but cognitive material can be made the carrier of a wide range of moods and emotions; conversely, one intended to transmit an affective state is bound to employ a cognitive medium. (The opposition of cognition and affection is, of course, a distinction brought about by the development of the cognitive aspects of human behaviour; it would be meaningless to apply it to the messages of creatures lacking this brand of sophistication.) In spite of these difficulties a start has been made in the study of the communication of emotional meaning with the important finding that sensitivity to the transmission of assumed emotion is related to cognitive but not to personality variables.

.   .   .

Throughout the book we have been concerned primarily with message from person to person. There are other highly important problems in human communication and it is desirable to give four of them quick mention.

First, self-communication. Before a message can be transmitted, it must be shaped and realized by the sender. The effort entailed in this depends partly on the skill of the sender and partly on the content of the message. If the message is the vehicle of deep and original content, its birth is likely to be the sequel to a complex gestation, during which ideas, facts and emotions have been brought together, organized, dissolved and reassembled perhaps many times over. This theme was touched on in the chapters on scientific research and creative art; it is hoped that enough was said to suggest the structural involvement of these processes, the difficulty of subjecting them to experimental study and the risks of trying to account for them over-simply. The material discussed in this book may perhaps supply some kind of groundwork to the study of creative processes, but it would be presumptuous to claim more. Perhaps it should be added that whereas the normal function of communication is to increase the receiver's store of information, that of the creative message goes further, modifying and extending the consciousness of the receiver. Indirect evidence of this is found in the effect of art—and music in particular—in releasing the hearer's or viewer's own creative potential.

Another neglected area is group communication. Groups are made up of individuals—as few as two (dyads), as many as the Chinese or Indians. Communications are made by individuals in the name of groups, to individuals in the name of groups, and from one group to another group. Topics of importance include the formation of group attitudes and the taking of group decisions. Such attitudes and decisions will be largely the product of communications between group members, and it is of concern to know the sort of individual who communicates most effectively, the types of communication that exert the strongest influence, and the kinds of group structure (whether formal or informal) that promote the most successful communication. Cognate themes are the moulding and manipulation of public opinion, and the mechanics of rumour.

Thirdly, we have been concerned throughout with *bona fide*

communication, ignoring the uses that can be made of communication over and above the transmission of information for its own sake. It was stated at one point that the purpose of communication appeared to be irrelevant to the mechanisms of transmission, and this would seem to be broadly true. It is, however, probable that individuals vary in their perceptiveness of a sender's motives, and it would be valuable to know more about the cues which make an utterance plausible or implausible, or which help us to discriminate plausibility from sincerity.

Finally, what of the human being as communicator? How does he stand in relation to other species? Does he possess undeveloped powers or powers that have atrophied from disuse? Has he rivals in the animal world? What has enabled him to develop the powers he has?

The standard answer to this type of question would perhaps be on the lines that the human being discovered articulate speech and later learned to record it in writing; that with the help of language he developed generalized thinking, which he refined into an instrument of dialectic; that twenty centuries of argument, which began as high intellectual exercise and descended slowly to the plains of logic-chopping aridity, were terminated by the discovery of the controlled experiment and the mathematics of process; and that these led in turn (and among many other things) to quickened communication through the invention of world-ranging vehicles and to its extension through the discovery of new media. Opinions would perhaps be divided as to the motive force behind this evolution, but few probably would deny that utility, necessity and fear have played a very considerable part in it. Nowhere has this been more obvious than in the stimulus given by the last war to communications research. At the same time it would be hard to dispute that, though the main effect of each stage may have been outgoing, a fair proportion of the human libido released has been turned inwards to reflection and imaginative construction. From time to time the balance of this outward inward division undergoes adjustment, as though in response to some hidden cybernetic principle. At the moment the outward direction appears to be favoured to a degree that makes living somewhat hazardous to those of schizoid temper.

The sensitivity of some species to messages of smell, vibration and ultra-sonic sources suggests that the human being, in his pursuit of the articulate, may have sacrificed other modes of communication. This possibility is made greater by the experiences of hyper-sensitive individuals, which, though hard to repeat in experimental conditions, are not invariably reduced to dust by interrogation, and which the enlightened worker will always look to for an extension of knowledge rather than resent as a challenge to his beliefs.

As for the conditions that make human communication possible, the reader is referred to a paper by J. C. Lilly (66) of the Communication Research Institute, Miami, Florida, who has for some years been studying tursiops truncatus (the bottle-nosed dolphin). The paper is entitled 'Critical brain size and language' and it examines the hypothesis that there is a critical, absolute brain size below which language, as we know it, is impossible, and above which it is possible and even probable. In the case of human infants acquisition of the basic elements of speech occur when the brain size is in the region of 900 to 1,000 grams. The brain of the infant tursiops reaches this size soon after birth and achieves the precise clicking of the adult at the same age.

The question arises: does tursiops possess a natural language or can he acquire an artificial one? On the latter point it has been found that electrical stimulation of certain brain areas elicit vocalizations in the air. The details of the experiments are given in a further paper, 'Operant conditioning of the bottlenose dolphin with electrical stimulation of the brain', published in the *Journal of Comparative and Physiological Psychology*. Since the publication of this in 1962 the author claims to have demonstrated that the dolphin can be trained to emit airborne sounds, that he can use these sounds in complex relationship with man, and that with proper training techniques it is possible to shape the vocalization to close copies of sounds that one wishes the dolphin to emit. As for the spontaneous use of these facilities, there is no doubt that the dolphin emits distress calls to its colleagues who appear to receive specific information about the action they are required to take. Lilly and his co-workers further report that their basic assumptions and expectations determine within limits the results attained by the animal. Thus, if the latter's vocalizations are ignored they will soon cease, but if the worker starts to expect vocalizations they are resumed.

The dolphin's intelligence and quasi-human characteristics

P

appear to have been recognized as early as the seventh century B.C., the period ascribed to the semi-legendary figure of Arion, poet of Corinth and inventor of the dithyramb, a hymn form in honour of the god Dionysus. Arion, it is related, had completed a highly successful tour of Magna Graecia, and boarded a vessel at Tarentum to return home. The ship sailed, and Arion, standing on deck among his trophies, found himself surrounded by a crew plotting murder and loot. Accepting the situation, the poet obtained permission to sing a last song, after which he plunged headlong into the water, where he was saved by a dolphin who had followed the ship enchanted by his music. Eastward they sped across the glittering sea, and the guilty crew strained after them, astonished at the harmony between man and beast.

Glossary

AFFECTIVE Relating to feeling or emotion; non-cognitive. It is important to distinguish the affective judgement from the affective message (or information). The latter aims to communicate the quality of affective experience, the former to convey cognitive information derived from it.

ALPHABET Any set of elements from which messages can be constructed. In a closed system the set of elements is predetermined and cannot be varied; in an open system (e.g. human language) some degree of variation can occur: words can be added or discarded, the meanings of words extended or contracted as the human being's exploration of his environment demands.

ASSUMPTION A taking for granted, e.g. that a piece of information or the meaning of a word is in the possession of the person addressed and therefore does not need to be stated.

ATTITUDE A generalization based on affective experience, rather as the concept is on cognitive experience. The main unit of affective judgement.

BEHAVIOURAL Relating to any aspect of human or animal response or activity, particularly those observable by a non-participant witness.

BIT (Binary digit) The choice between two equally probable possibilities. When the outcome of such a situation (e.g. the tossing of a coin) becomes known, one bit of information is acquired. Where the probabilities are unequal but known, acquisition can be expressed in terms (fractions) of bits. Information of this type can be viewed as the removal of uncertainty. There are very few life situations where acquired information can be measured in this sense, although the concept of uncertainty reduction can sometimes be applied qualitatively, as when the possibilities in a guessing game are systematically eliminated.

CAPACITY The capacity of a communication channel is measured by the number of bits per second that can be transmitted. By analogy we may think of the central nervous system as a channel of limited capaicity (cf. load, span of apprehension). This is a fruitful

227

analogy, provided the many complexities of the human system are not lost sight of, e.g. the interplay of different sensory modalities, the many varieties of distraction (noise), and the resources by which the human being often appears to transcend load limitation.

CLOSED SYSTEM   A system with a finite alphabet or number of elements. The conditions of closure in a communication system presuppose that the elements cannot acquire extended application as they do in human language. In other words, closed systems cannot be made the vehicles of direct meaning or expression.

CODING   A telegraphic code is a set of letter, figure or word groups to which arbitrary meanings have been assigned for purposes of brevity or secrecy. It is essential that those using the code shall have full knowledge of the relation between symbols and meanings. Something analogous occurs when the stimuli impinging on an organism give rise to perception, and whenever information is transmitted, whether by speech, writing or any other medium.

COMMUNICATION THEORY   Initially a model which enables the engineer to structure his conceptions of the changes through which an electrical signal passes, beginning as input and ending as output. To be distinguished from information theory, which is a technique of measurement for assessing the fidelity with which signals imposed on a channel are transformed into outputs.

CONCEPT   A generalized cognitive notion (cf. attitude). The ability to form concepts is of comparatively late development in the individual, and may be viewed as a device for transcending the experience of the moment. Concepts can be regarded as abstractions from perceptual experiences linked by a single common factor, though it is not established beyond doubt that they originate in this way. The penalty of conceptual thinking lies in disregard for the uniqueness of the particular instance.

CONNOTATION   A logical term used to denote the subject and at the same time imply its attributes. In the language of the present discussion a sign message denotes but has no connotation, whereas a content message denotes and connotes. A term's range of attributes permits selectivity by both sender and receiver and so opens the door to ambiguity in discourse.

CONTENT INFORMATION   Information which connotes as well as denotes, which, in everyday language, conveys meaning. Because a word's connotation makes selectivity possible (the word may convey one or two only of several attributes), there can be no guarantee that a correct use of words will ensure understanding. For this to be ensured the speaker would need to know the receiver's state of information as well as the word's full range of meaning. These conditions are rarely met.

DECODING The process of converting a coded message back into its original form.

ENTROPY The entropy of statistical mechanics measures the uncertainty as to which of many possible states a physical system is actually in. In communication theory, the entropy concept is applied to the average uncertainty as to what element the source will produce next. This entropy, measured in bits per element or bits per second, is equal to the average number of binary digits needed to transmit messages produced by the source. Other things being equal, the choice between two proposed systems will fall upon the one with the lower entropy.

INCOMPATIBILITY Literally 'inability to suffer with'. Used here of mutually inconsistent bases of interpretation for given messages.

INFORMATION A term to cover any type of message (sign, content or affective) transmissible from sender to receiver.

INFORMATION THEORY A mathematical technique for measuring the effectiveness of sign transmission in a man-made system. What is measured is the speed or economy with which sign information (uncertainty reduction) can be brought about.

INPUT What is fed into a transmission system.

MEANING This word has both psychological and linguistic references. The latter, exhaustively analysed by Ogden and Richards, is concerned with the relation between word and designated object; the former, now being explored under the head of semantic differential, is specially concerned with verbal connotation, inter-sensory associations and contractions of verbal application. In addition, meaning implies a conscious subject, for whom the elements of a closed system possess fixed meaning while those in an open system are dynamic.

MECHANISM Used initially of a machine with interrelated parts and operations; in psychology applied metaphorically (a) to a semi-automatic reaction pattern issuing from repressed emotional complexes (e.g. defence mechanism), and (b) of any established relationship underlying observed behaviour.

MECHANOMORPHISM A term coined for the tendency to interpret the behaviour of living creatures in terms of the operations of a man-made machine.

MEDIUM Any instrument for transmitting information, whether a human sense or combination of senses, or a natural or man-made vehicle of transmission. Every medium is selective in respect of the material it transmits so that 'accounts' given by two media are never identical.

MODEL A representation of a process made with the intention of submitting a hypothesis to experimental trial. The originators of scientific and mathematical models seek to select the essential and discard the irrelevant features of observed situations, thereby hoping to reduce the unmanageably complicated to testable form. All technical terms require interpretation in the light of the models which gave rise to them.

NOISE   Any undesired disturbance in a communication system such as random electrical currents. Noise is observed as hissing in a radio receiver and as white flecks (snow) on a television screen. In human communication any source of message distortion from unwanted sound to distracting emotions by the receiver may be thought of analogically as noise.

OPEN SYSTEM   A system whose alphabet or set of basic elements can be added to or developed after the manner of human language.

OUTPUT   The elements that come out of a transmission system. Elements lost in transit between input and output are normally the casualties of noise.

PERCEPTION   The process of becoming aware of some feature or aspect of the environment. A perception represents a transaction between the subject and the external world which the former acquires largely by learning. Once learned, a perception may regress to the level of a habit, but can be reactivated by conscious effort or a change in the environment.

PERIPHERAL VARIATION   The subjective elements of connotative meaning as compared with the central elements on which there is fairly general agreement.

PHONEME   A speech sound. The number of such sounds that human beings can articulate runs into hundreds, but each language is built around a small selection, usually between twenty and forty. The main classes of phoneme are termed vowels, fricatives, stops and resonants, each group being defined by some specific use of the speech organs.

PROPRIOCEPTIVE   Related to, originated by a receptor or sense-organ situated within the body's tissues, e.g. proprioceptive cues.

PROCESSING   The phrase information processing derives from the transmission of signs in a closed system. A system with a high transmission rate is said to process effectively and vice versa. The concept can be applied with fair accuracy to the human being's handling of material relevant to a closed system, e.g. the calling out of letters or numerals, and the manipulation of well-learned operations like the four arithmetical processes. While processing clearly plays a part in all mental activity, it appears largely irrelevant to learning situations and what are loosely known as the higher mental functions. Its relevance would appear to be inversely related to the creative component of mental activity.

REDUNDANCY With sign information the occurrence of a sign which does not influence expectation of its successors is said to lack redundancy. In this context redundancy is equivalent to loaded probability; it is minimal where probabilities are independent, maximal where dependency nears completion (for example, in a recurring decimal). In the transcription of English text the appearance of a letter will to some degree influence the expectation of subsequent characters. In spoken or written language redundancy increases with the acquisition of meaning, but in the everyday sense we only speak of redundancy when words add nothing to meaning already obtained. In a more technical sense all forms of emphasis can be regarded as energic redundancy, the term here being used to describe the means of stressing what is valuable or important to the speaker. Finally, in aesthetics, redundancy can be employed as an instrument of pleasure, e.g. a musical line of poetry is usually found on analysis to present a pattern of carefully selected sounds involving repetition.

SCHEMA Conceived initially as a mental framework derived from past experience and influencing the interpretation of the new. Taken over and given a neurological slant by Head, who saw the body-image as a proto-schema. Reintroduced to psychology by Bartlett and used currently as a descriptive term for all mental predispositions (supposedly but not observably with neural correlates) which assist us in assimilating fresh material. In this sense some schemas are found to be incompatible, and much failure of communication is due to the existence of incompatible schemas in sender and receiver. Some schemas are 'good' in that they can absorb a wide range of material, whereas 'bad' schemas are resistant to new content.

SEMANTIC To do with verbal meaning—as compared with syntactic, which is concerned with verbal arrangement and the construction of sentences.

SEMANTIC DIFFERENTIAL A statistical (factorial) technique for identifying the elements or dimensions contributing to verbal meaning and offering a means of comparing the meanings assigned to cognitive or affective notions by different groups or individuals.

SIGN Initially a mark used conventionally to denote something other than itself. In this sense most words begin as signs, but through association and the interplay of different sense modalities they become invested with meaning. Throughout this book the word sign is used only of marks that do not acquire extended meaning, that is, of the elements of the alphabets of closed systems.

SIGN INFORMATION Messages composed of signs.

SIGNAL A sign or group of signs deliberately transmitted.

SUB-BEHAVIOURAL Relating to components of human or animal

activities (responses) that do not differentiate agent or action, e.g. the relative incidence of different letters of the alphabet as found in the texts of different writers. These incidences tend to be unvarying from writer to writer and from one type of subject matter to another.

SYNAESTHAESIA   Used of sensations in one sense modality which carry impressions or can be expressed in terms of another (e.g. the ascriptions of colour or visual form to sound). The phenomenon of synaesthaesia provided the starting-point of Osgood's exploration of the semantic differential.

SYNTACTIC   Relating to the ways in which words can be arranged and sentences constructed; contrasted with semantic, which is concerned with verbal meaning. Syntactics and semantics constitute the twin pillars of language study. Research is demonstrating that some types of common syntactic usage can retard or prevent communication as effectively as the use of obscure words.

SYSTEM   A collection of components or devices intended to perform some specified function or functions. The intensive study of the properties of engineering systems has led to the transfer of the term to human and social situations. Such transfer is legitimate so long as it is remembered that human beings and societies, unlike engineering systems, have not been designed for a small number of specific functions, but have evolved over vast periods of time in the course of which they have developed a capacity of response to an enormous range of situations.

TRANSMISSION   Literally a 'sending across or through'. Every message requires transmission, and the transmission of information invariably entails a medium. The conversion of information into a form in which it can travel is known as encoding, its subsequent reconversion as decoding. The code, like the alphabet, may be closed or open. A code devised to carry out a specific function is likely to be of the first sort, which alone can ensure full freedom from ambiguity.

UNCERTAINTY REDUCTION   The prime attribute of sign information; it is expressible mathematically in bits.

WHITE NOISE   Noise in which all frequencies in a given band have equal powers.

Bibliography

1 ABERCROMBIE, M. L. *The Anatomy of Judgment*. London: Hutchinson, 1960.

2 ALLAN, M. D. 'Perceptual organization and its relation to training in perceptual skills.' Paper to British Psychological Society, 1959.

3 AVERBACH, E. and SPERLING, G. 'Short-term storage of information in vision.' Paper to London Conference on Information Theory, 1960.

4 BARBER, C. *The Story of Language*. London: Pan Books, 1964.

5 BARTLETT, F. C. *Remembering*. Cambridge: Cambridge University Press, 1932.

6 BELDOCH, S. 'Sensitivity to emotional expressions in three modes of communication.' In DAVITZ, J. R. (ed.) *The Communication of Emotional Meaning*. New York: McGraw-Hill, 1964.

7 BLACK, J. W. 'Language barriers and language training.' In GELDARD, F. A. (ed.) *Communication Processes*. Oxford: Pergamon Press, 1965.

8 BREMERMANN, H. J. 'The evolution of intelligence: the nervous system as a model of its environment.' Paper for U.S. Navy, 1958 (University of Washington Contract.)

9 BROADBENT, D. E. *Perception and Communication*. London: Pergamon Press, 1958.

10 BROADBENT, D. E. 'A study of short-term memory in old and young people.' Paper to British Psychological Society. (Abstract in *BPS Bulletin*, January 1961.)

11 BROADBENT, D. E. 'Flow of information within the organism.' *Journal of Verbal Learning and Verbal Behaviour*, Vol. 2, No. 1, 1963.

12 BROADBENT, D. E. 'The choice of words and the choice of actions.' Paper to British Psychological Society. (Abstract in *BPS Bulletin*, April 1964.)

13 BROADBENT, D. E. 'Signal transmission: factors within the human operator in communication.' In GELDARD, F. A. (ed.) *Communication Processes*. Oxford: Pergamon Press, 1965.

14 BROADBENT, D. E. 'Information theory and older approaches in Psychology.' Applied Psychology Research Unit paper, 1958.

233

15 BROADBENT, D. E. 'Techniques for the study of short-term memory.' Paper to British Psychological Society. (Abstract in *BPS Bulletin*, April 1964.)

16 BROADBENT, D. E. 'How noise affects work.' *New Society*, 3 March 1966.

17 BURT, C. 'Test construction and the scaling of items.' *British Journal of Statistical Psychology*, October 1951, 95–129.

18 BURT, C. 'The concept of consciousness.' *British Journal of Psychology*, August 1962.

19 BURT, C., COOPER, W. F. and MARTIN, J. L. 'A psychological study of typography.' *British Journal of Statistical Psychology*, 1955.

20 CARNAP, R. 'Philosophy and logical syntax.' In WHITE, M. *The Age of Analysis: 20th Century Philosophers*. New American Library, 1955.

21 CHAPANIS, A. 'Men, machines and models.' Paper to British Psychological Society. (Abstract in *BPS Bulletin*, January 1961.)

22 CHAPANIS, A. 'Words, words, words.' *Human Factors*, March 1965.

23 CHASE, S. *The Tyranny of Words*. London: Methuen, 1950.

24 CHERRY, C. '"Communication theory" and human behaviour.' In SMITH, A. H. and QUIRK, R. (eds.) *Studies in Communication*. London: Secker & Warburg, 1955.

25 CHERRY, C. 'On the validity of applying communication theory to experimental psychology.' *British Journal of Psychology*, August 1957.

26 CHOMSKY, N. *Syntactic Structure*. The Hague: Mouton, 1957.

27 CHOMSKY, N. *Current Issues in Linguistic Theory*. The Hague: Mouton, 1964.

28 CONRAD, R. 'The design of information.' *Occupational Psychology*, July 1962.

29 COOMBS, C. H. 'A theory of psychological scaling.' *Engineering Research Institute Bulletin*, No. 34. Ann Arbor: University of Michigan Press, 1952.

30 CROSSMAN, E. R. F. W. 'Information and order in human immediate memory.' Paper to London Conference on Information Theory, 1960.

31 CROSSMAN, E. R. F. W. 'Information and noise in the human brain.' Paper to British Psychological Society. (Abstract in *BPS Bulletin*, October 1963.)

32 CROWTHER, J. G. 'When "scientist" was new.' *New Scientist*, 3 March 1966.

33 CUNNINGHAM, C. 'Forensic psychology, a novel application.' *British Psychological Society Bulletin*, January 1964.

34 DAVITZ, J. R. *The Communication of Emotional Meaning.* New York: McGraw-Hill, 1964.

35 EMPSON, W. *Seven Types of Ambiguity.* London: Chatto and Windus, 1953.

36 FODOR, J. A. and KATZ, J. F. (eds.) *The Structure of Language: Readings in the Philosophy of Language.* New York: Prentice Hall, 1964.

37 GARDINER, H. W. 'The 1964 British and American elections: a semantic differential assessment of political concepts.' Paper to British Psychological Society. (Abstract in *BPS Bulletin,* April 1965.)

38 GELDARD, F. A. (ed.) *Communication Processes.* Oxford: Pergamon Press, 1965.

39 GLANZER, M. (University of Maryland.) 'Coding and use of information in problem-solving.' Project paper, 1963.

40 GOFFMAN, E. *The Presentation of Self in Everyday Life.* University of Edinburgh: Monograph, 1956.

41 GOLDMAN EISLER, F. 'Hesitation and information in speech.' Paper to London Conference on Information Theory, 1960.

42 GOLDSMITH, M. 'The communication of scientific ideas.' Address to First Bath Conference: Technology and Society, 1965.

43 GOWERS, E. *Plain Words.* London: H.M. Stationery Office, 1948.

44 GREGORY, C. C. L. 'A proposal to replace belief by method in the pre-mensural sciences.' Letter to *Nature,* 9 January 1960.

45 GUILBAUD, G. T. *What is Cybernetics?* London: Hutchinson, 1959.

46 HARDING, D. W. 'The poetry of Sir Thomas Wyatt.' *Scrutiny,* 1946.

47 HAWARD, L. R. C. 'Forensic psychology.' *British Psychological Society Bulletin,* January 1961.

48 HAWARD, L. R. C. 'Psychological experiments and judicial doubt.' Paper to British Psychological Society. (Abstract in *BPS Bulletin,* January 1964.)

49 HELLER, E. *The Disinherited Mind* (essay on Goethe and the Idea of Scientific Truth). Harmondsworth: Penguin Books, 1961.

50 HICK, W. E. 'Information theory and intelligence tests.' *British Journal of Statistical Psychology,* 1951.

51 HICK, W. E. 'On the rate of gain of information.' *Quarterly Journal of Experimental Psychology,* 1952.

52 HOGGART, R. *The Uses of Literacy.* London: Chatto and Windus, 1957.

53 HOGGART, R. 'Values and virtues.' Address to First Bath Conference: Technology and Society, 1965.

54 HOTOPF, W. H. N. 'Perception and the use of language.' Paper to British Psychological Society. (Abstract in *BPS Bulletin,* May 1961.)

55 HUDSON, L. 'Creativity and intelligence.' Paper to British Psychological Society, Education section. (Abstract in *BPS Bulletin*, January 1964.)

56 HUNTER, D. 'Computers at war.' *New Scientist*, 3 March 1966.

57 IZARD, C. E. and TOMKINS, S. S. 'Affect and behaviour: anxiety as a negative affect.' In SPIELBERGER, E. D. (ed.) *Anxiety and Behaviour*. New York: Academic Press, 1966.

58 JONES, S. 'Why can't leaflets be logical?' *New Society*, 10 September 1964.

59 KANTOROVICH, M. 'Thoughts at a distance.' Abstract of Russian paper, 1964.

60 KAY, H. 'Channel capacity and skilled performance.' Paper to NATO Symposium of Military Psychology, 1960.

61 KELVIN, R. P. 'What sort of people?' *New Society*, 9, 16 and 23 May, 1963.

62 KOESTLER, A. *The Act of Creation*. London: Hutchinson, 1964.

63 LEONARD, J. A. 'A reconsideration of the early history of reaction time studies.' Applied Psychology Research Unit paper, 1953.

64 LEONARD, J. A. 'Choice reaction time experiments and information theory.' Applied Psychology Research Unit paper, 1960.

65 LEVY, P. K. 'Ability to express and perceive vocal communication of feeling.' In DAVITZ, J. R. (ed.) *The Communication of Emotional Meaning*. New York: McGraw-Hill, 1964.

66 LILLY, J. C. 'Communication studies on tursiops truncatus.' Abstract report on U.S. Navy project at Communication Research Institute, Miami, Florida, 1964.

67 LILLY, R. S. 'A development study of the semantic differential.' Report on project at Princeton University, Princeton, New Jersey, 1965.

68 LLOYD, D. *The Idea of Law*. Harmondsworth: Penguin Books, 1964.

69 LOVELL, K. 'The philosophy of Jean Piaget.' *New Society*, 11 August 1966.

70 MACKAY, D. M. 'The informational analysis of questions and commands.' Paper to London Conference on Information Theory, 1960.

71 MCCLELLAND, D. C. *The Roots of Consciousness*. New York: Van Nostrand, 1964.

72 MCGEE, V. E. 'Non-verbal speech factors.' Report on research project at Dartmouth College, 1966.

73 MCLUHAN, M. *Understanding Media*. London: Routledge & Kegan Paul, 1965.

74 MACPHERSON, S. *Form in Music* (Chapter 18). London: Joseph Williams Ltd, 1930.

75 MEREDITH, P. *Learning, Remembering and Knowing.* London: English Universities Press Ltd, 1961.

76 MILLER, G. A. *Language and Communication.* New York: McGraw-Hill, 1963.

77 MILLER, G. A. 'What is information measurement?' *American Psychologist,* Vol. 8, 1953.

78 MILLER, G. A. 'Some psychological studies of grammar.' *American Psychologist,* Vol. 17, 1962.

79 MORRIS, C. *Signification and Significance: A Study of the Relations of Signs and Values.* Massachusetts Institute of Technology Press, 1964.

80 OGDEN, C. K. and RICHARDS, I. A. *The Meaning of Meaning.* London: Kegan Paul, 1923.

81 OLDFIELD, R. C. and ZANGWILL, O. L. 'Head's concept of the schema and its application in contemporary British psychology.' *British Journal of Psychology,* 1942 and 1943.

82 OSGOOD, C. E. 'The nature and measurement of meaning.' *Psychological Bulletin,* May 1952.

83 OSGOOD, C. E., SUCI, G. J. and TANNENBAUM, P. H. *The Measurement of Meaning.* Urbana: University of Illinois Press, 1957.

84 PACKARD, V. *The Hidden Persuaders.* Harmondsworth: Penguin Books, 1960.

85 PARRY, J. 'Planned sampling as an aid to objectivity in literary criticism.' Paper to British Psychological Society, 1947.

86 PIAGET, J. *The Child's Conception of the World.* London: Kegan Paul, 1929.

87 PIAGET, J. *Les Mécanismes Perceptifs.* Paris: Presses Universitaires de France, 1961.

88 PIERCE, J. R. *Symbols, Signals and Noise: The Nature and Process of Communication.* London: Hutchinson, 1962.

89 POULTON, E. C. *Effects of Printing Types and Formats on the Comprehension of Scientific Journals.* Cambridge: Cambridge University Press, 1959.

90 REYNOLDS, D. and ROSENBLATT, R. D. *Short-term Memory: An Annotated Bibliography.* HUMRRO Division No. 1, 1965.

91 SCHRODER, J. H. and BLACKMAN, S. 'The measurement of conceptual dimensions.' Report of Princeton University project, 1965.

92 SHANNON, C. E. and WEAVER, W. *The Mathematical Theory of Communication.* Urbana: University of Illinois Press, 1949.

93 SKEMP, R. R. 'The need for a schematic learning theory.' *British Journal of Educational Psychology,* June 1962.

94 STANFORD, C. V. *Musical Composition.* London: Macmillan, 1911.

95 STANILAND, A. C. *Patterns of Redundancy.* Cambridge: Cambridge University Press, 1966.

96 STICHMAN, E. P. and RENAUD, G. E. 'Information extraction from voice communications: work methods for single transcribers.' U.S. Army Personnel Research Office, Technical Research Note No. 154, 1965.

97 SUMMERFIELD, A. and LEGGE, D. 'Perception and information theory.' *British Psychological Society Bulletin*, September 1960.

98 TEAR, D. H., TURNER, S. H. and WALLACE, W. H. 'How previous experience affects response in ambiguous situations.' Report on University of Pennsylvania project, 1963.

99 TEICHNER, W. H. 'Information processing under task stress.' Report on USAF project (Decision Sciences Laboratories, Bedford, Mass.), 1963.

100 TURNER, S. H., WALLACE, W. H. and WESSEL, A. E. 'Errors in information processing by human beings.' Report on University of Pennsylvania project, 1963.

101 VALENTINE, C. W. *The Experimental Psychology of Beauty*. London: Methuen, 1962.

102 VERNON, M. D. 'The function of schemata in perceiving.' *Psychological Review*, 1955.

103 VERNON, M. D. *The Psychology of Perception*. Harmondsworth: Penguin Books, 1962.

104 VICINO, F. L., ANDREWS, R. S. and RINGEL, S. 'Conspicuity coding of updated symbolic information.' U.S. Army Personnel Research Office, Technical Research Note No. 152, 1965.

105 WASON, P. C. 'Psychological aspects of negation: an experimental enquiry and some practical applications.' Communication Research Centre, University College, London, 1962.

106 WASON, P. C. 'The processing of positive and negative information.' *Quarterly Journal of Experimental Psychology*, May 1959.

107 WASON, P. C. 'Response to affirmative and negative binary statements.' *British Journal of Psychology*, 1961.

108 WEBSTER, T. B. L. 'Communication of thought in Ancient Greece.' In SMITH, A. H. and QUIRK, R. (eds.) *Studies in Communication*. London: Secker & Warburg, 1955.

109 WEISZ, A. Z. and MCELROY, L. S. 'Information processing in a complex task under speed stress.' Report on USAF project (Decision Sciences Laboratories, Bedford, Mass.), 1963.

110 WEISZ, A. Z., LICKLIDER, J. C. R., SWETS, J. A. and WILSON, J. P. 'Human pattern recognition procedures as related to military recognition problems.' Report by Bolt, Beranek and Newman for USAF, 1962.

111 WERTHEIMER, M. *Productive Thinking*. New York: Harper and Bros, 1959.

112 WHITE, M. *The Age of Analysis: 20th Century Philosophers*. New American Library, 1955.

113 WIEGAND, K. L. 'Uncertainty as a fundamental variable in three kinds of information processing tasks.' Project report, USAF, AMRL, 1963.

114 WIENER, N. *Cybernetics*. New York: John Wiley and Sons, 1948.

115 WITTGENSTEIN, L. *Tractatus Logico-Philosophicus*. London: Kegan Paul, 1921.

116 WITTGENSTEIN, L. *Philosophical Investigations*. Oxford: Blackwell, 1959.

117 YOUNG, J. Z. 'The influence of language on medicine.' In SMITH, A. H. and QUIRK, R. (eds.) *Studies in Communication*. London: Secker & Warburg, 1955.

118 YOUNG, J. Z. *A Model of the Brain*. Oxford: Clarendon Press, 1965.

119 YULE, G. U. *The Statistical Study of Literary Vocabulary*. Cambridge: Cambridge University Press, 1946.

Index